# Created Equal

The Palgrave Macmillan series, in association with Amnesty International, illuminates the greatest human rights issues facing the world today. From human trafficking to poverty, terrorism to freedom of expression, this dynamic and accessible series encourages debate about the situation today and the path we took to get here, allowing people with many different perspectives to tell their own stories of struggle.

# Created Equal

## Voices on Women's Rights

*Anna Horsbrugh-Porter*

palgrave
macmillan

*For Ella, Hal, Minna, and Louis*

CREATED EQUAL
Copyright © Amnesty International UK, 2009.
All rights reserved.
17–25 New Inn Yard, London EC2A 3EA, UK
www.amnesty.org.uk

The views expressed in this book do not necessarily reflect the
views of Amnesty International.

First published in 2009 by PALGRAVE MACMILLAN® in
the U.S.—a division of St. Martin's Press LLC, 175 Fifth
Avenue, New York, NY 10010.

Where this book is distributed in the UK, Europe and the rest
of the world, this is by Palgrave Macmillan, a division of
Macmillan Publishers Limited, registered in England, company
number 785998, of Houndmills, Basingstoke, Hampshire
RG21 6XS.

Palgrave Macmillan is the global academic imprint of the above
companies and has companies and representatives throughout
the world.

Palgrave® and Macmillan® are registered trademarks in the
United States, the United Kingdom, Europe and other
countries.

ISBN-13: 978-0-230-61733-9

Library of Congress Cataloging-in-Publication Data
Horsbrugh Porter, Anna, 1965–
    Created equal : voices on women's rights / Anna Horsbrugh-
Porter.
        p.   cm.
    Includes bibliographical references and index.
    ISBN 0-230-61733-6
    1. Women's rights.   2. Women—History.   I. Title.
HQ1236.H67   2009
305.42—dc22

                                                              2009022875

A catalogue record of the book is available from the British
Library.

Design by Letra Libre

First edition: September 2009
10  9  8  7  6  5  4  3  2  1
Printed in the United States of America.

# Contents

*Foreword*                                    vii
 —Patrick Stewart
*Introduction*                                 xi

1. **Education and Work**                        1

   A Woman's Place Is in the Home              2
   Education for All                          10
   Public Space                               16
   Virtual Slavery                            24
   Sticky Floors                              30
   Half the Sky                               37

2. **Wives and Daughters**                      45

   I Do                                       45
   Breaking the Silence                       52
   Sex outside Marriage                       61
   Female Genital Mutilation                  69
   Widows and Witches                         77
   Women in Prison                            84

**3.  Health**                                         91

Maternal Health                                        91
Contraception                                          96
Abortion                                              101

**4.  Sex**                                           107

Threadlifts, Skin Peels, and Internal Bras           107
Women and War                                        110
On the Game                                          119
X-rated                                              126

**5.  Poverty**                                       133

Environment and Gender                               134
Globalization                                        138
Women Refugees                                       145

**6.  Making Changes**                                153

Activism                                             153
Keeping the Peace                                    160
A Level Playing Field                                164
Justice for All                                      171

*Notes*                                               180
*Sources and Suggestions for Further Information*     192
*Index*                                               198

# Foreword

Women's rights—which are utterly fundamental human rights—are denied and violated in a multitude of ways all over the world. This repression of life affects us all, whether we acknowledge it or not, and *Created Equal* provides tremendous insights into the many faces of prejudice, and the inequality and horrors to which they can lead.

When women are denied their rights as equal human beings, it leads with great inevitability to frustration, unhappiness, pain, and, in all too many cases, violence. I experienced first-hand violence against my mother from an angry and unhappy man who was not able to control his emotions or his hands. Great harm was done by those events—and of course I mean the physical harm, the physical scars that were left, the blood that was spilled, the wounds that were exposed—but there were also other aspects of violence which have had a lasting impact psychologically on family members. It is so destructive and tainting.

It's taken me a long time to be able to speak about what happened. Then, around the time of the launch of the Amnesty International campaign to Stop Violence

Against Women, all that changed. After consultation with my brothers, we all felt that it was time for me to speak out about what had happened in our childhood, and to show people that domestic violence is protected by silence.

As a child witnessing these events, one cannot help somehow feeling responsible for the pain and screaming and misery. It is deeply confusing, and these confusions are not things which are easily disposed of in adult life. They stay with you. Any child exposed to such lack of self control, intimidation, turmoil, and chaos is given a very bad lesson in male responsibility and self governance.

Violence against women is a worldwide phenomenon, one which in some countries is much more severe and destructive then anything I experienced. This is the reason why Amnesty International's work to bring people's attention to the issue is so important, because it is here among us and it is continuing in the world at large. As far as the authorities are concerned there have been great advances—and there needed to be, because as a child I heard police officers in my own home saying "well, she must have provoked him," and doctors saying "well, Mrs. Stewart, it takes two to make a fight." Well, they had no idea.

Today we are more sensitive than that, but we are still not sensitive enough. Still these things are hushed up, still the violence is allowed to continue, still violence against women is normalized and glamorized by its constant depiction in films—and in particular, Hollywood films. I myself have been involved in sequences, both in the theatre and in film, which, with hindsight, I realized were offensive because they were perpetuating a stereotype. It's so irresponsible to perpetuate the violent attitudes of men to women.

One way this deeply troubling element in modern life can be opposed is through government intervention. According to the United Nations, one of every three women in the world today will experience physical or sexual abuse. That's why I would like to see these issues being taken as seriously by governments. Violence against women diminishes us all. If you fail to raise your hand in protest, then you make yourself part of the problem.

We need to recognize that violence against women is a symptom of a much bigger problem: that women's rights are systematically ignored and abused. After all, it is so much harder to inflict pain and injustice on an equal than it is on someone we view as a lesser human being. And ultimately, to deny women their equal rights, to dehumanize them on any level, retards humankind. Dip into any chapter of this book and we can find real scope for change, for betterment, for fulfillment of women's lives and rights. I cannot stress enough how important this is.

—*Patrick Stewart*

# Introduction

*Violence against women is perhaps the most shameful human rights violation. And it is perhaps the most pervasive. It knows no boundaries of geography, culture, or wealth. As long as it continues we cannot claim to be making real progress towards equality, development and peace.*

—Kofi Annan, former secretary general
of the United Nations[1]

All human beings are entitled to basic rights, but women and girl children are not treated the same as men and boy children. Millions of women throughout the world suffer violence, poverty, and denial of their human rights for no other reason than their gender. This book looks at women's lives all over the world to find out what happens when their rights are violated, but also to learn what can be achieved when their rights are protected and equality upheld.

Wherever you go in the world, a minimum of one in four women are denied their human rights. If you take an average sample of the global population, a village of 1,000 people, this is how it would break down:

- 500 people are women (It would be 510, but 10 women were never born because of gender-selective abortion or because they died of neglect in infancy);
- 167 of the women will be beaten or exposed to some form of violence during their lifetime;
- 100 women will be victims of rape or attempted rape during their lifetime.

In general, civil societies all over the world, with their differing educational, legal, and welfare systems, are still predominantly set up and administered by men. The result is that fundamental and inalienable women's rights are neither integral to society nor constitutionally guaranteed, but remain as a bonus, an add-on, something that can be taken away or dispensed with rapidly in times of stress and external pressures. At the beginning of the twenty-first century, women remain largely excluded from decision making and legal processes on both a national and an international level.

To change women's lives, it is crucial to educate women and girl children about their rights and to give them the means to become autonomous decision makers. It is also vital to educate men. Those who hold power in civil society—judges, police officers, government officials, property owners, employers, educators, and religious leaders—must be made to realize the value and importance of women's rights. This involves their taking responsibility for their own attitudes and assumptions and educating their sons about the necessity of a true and lasting equality.

Legislating for women's rights was a gradual process throughout the twentieth century. In 1933 the Convention on the Nationality of Women was adopted at the Seventh International Conference of American States in Montevideo, Uruguay. It allowed a woman to retain her own nationality if she married a man of another nationality. This was the first international treaty ever adopted concerning the rights of women; it was also the first international conference that women were allowed to attend as part of the delegations.

Twelve years later, in 1945, the UN Charter, the founding document of the United Nations, affirmed the "equal rights of men and women," "the dignity and worth of the human person," and the realization of fundamental human rights for all as core UN principles and objectives.[2] Then, in 1979 came one of the most important international conferences on women's equality—the United Nations Convention on the Elimination of All Forms of Discrimination against Women (CEDAW). A legally binding treaty that dealt comprehensively with women's rights, it defined discrimination in the following way:

> Any distinction, exclusion or restriction made on the basis of sex which has the effect or purpose of impairing or nullifying the recognition, enjoyment or exercise by women, irrespective of their marital status, on a basis of equality of

> men and women, of human rights and funda-
> mental freedoms in the political, economic, so-
> cial, cultural, civil or any other field.[3]

The most valuable aspect of this convention was the critical accountability mechanism it included. When states ratify the CEDAW, they also assume responsibility for enshrining the principle of equality between men and women in their constitutions and legislative systems. In other words, they have to make sure that their laws are enforced.[4] In September 1995, the fourth United Nations World Conference on Women was held in Beijing and brought together 189 states and 2,600 nongovernmental organizations. The conference ended with the adoption of the Beijing Declaration and a "Platform for Action," which encouraged all signatory states to take specific legal and cultural measures to protect women's rights. Violence and the effects of armed conflict on women were specifically targeted as areas of concern.

This book assumes no prior knowledge on the reader's part, and it does not aim to be comprehensive. It is just a very small window into the lives of some of the 3 billion women living in the world today, a majority of whom are coping in difficult situations, trying to normalize life for their children, just trying to survive:

> The most important thing that anyone could do
> for us would be to help to collect the bodies that
> lie in the streets in front of our homes every
> morning, the ones that no one dares to touch,

> that our children see every day as we try to take them to school.
>
> —Iraqi women, when asked about their greatest concern, April 2007[5]

While this book predominantly looks at the lives of contemporary women, it is also important to remember how it all started: the struggle for emancipation that women undertook in the West at the beginning of the last century. Richard Pankhurst, the son of leading British suffragette Sylvia Pankhurst, recounts his mother's experience in 1913 when she was imprisoned for her involvement with the campaign to give women the right to vote:

> She describes how, having been hunger striking for three days, six men came in, thrust her onto a bed, held her hands and then two doctors came in with a metal instrument to open her teeth, thrust a pipe into her throat and pumped food into her stomach. Immediately she vomited but they came again in the evening, and so it went on, day after day, morning and evening, forcibly feeding her, until eventually she decided to adopt a sleep strike, she walked backwards day and night to stop herself from falling to sleep and to speed up her physical deterioration.[6]

# 1

# Education and Work

This section looks at women and their relationship to power both inside and outside the home. What areas of control have gender demarcations? What pressures, both cultural and religious, are exerted on women in terms of dress, conduct, education, and work? What happens when the traditional male hierarchy is overturned, when a woman is successful at work, in business, or in politics—and in some cases even takes the highest political office in the land?

Finally, and fundamentally, this section will address the fact that all activity outside the domestic sphere for women is predicated on ensuring the absolute human right to education. Girls and women can accomplish very little in a public space without it, and denying them a basic education is the surest way to keep them at home, out of sight and earshot.

## A Woman's Place Is in the Home—
## And What Happens When She Leaves It

*Woman is made specifically to please man.*

—Jean-Jacques Rousseau, 1762[1]

*Gentleness, docility, and a spaniel-like affection are . . .*
*consistently recommended as the cardinal virtues of the*
*sex . . . one writer has declared that it is masculine for a*
*woman to be melancholy. She was created to be the toy of*
*man, his rattle, and it must jingle in his ears whenever,*
*dismissing reason, he chooses to be amused.*

—Mary Wollstonecraft, 1792[2]

*131 Bellows for Dusting*
*When cleaning down, one of the handiest labour-savers is*
*a pair of bellows. In cleaning the head and foot of a wire*
*spring mattress, where the dust collects, a good pair of bel-*
*lows blows out the dust and fluff in a minute. For the*
*back of wardrobes that are too heavy to move stand at one*
*end and blow the bellows behind along the skirting board,*
*and you will find the dust out at the other end.*[3]

A pair of bellows and a passion for cleaning—this is a sur-
real picture of virtuous womanhood, conducting an ongoing war against the combined enemies of dust and dirt.
Always on a high state of alert for these domestic battles
fought on the home front: that is the traditional ideal of a
good woman, a safe woman, whose primary role is as a

housewife and mother. Modest, respectful, conforming in dress, speech, and behavior—a figurehead for her sex.

This tip about dusting is just one of over 30,000 entries submitted to The Good Housewife Competition run by the British Good Housekeeping Institute in the 1920s. Other entries ranged from the bizarre to the plainly unnecessary:

> *How to Sweeten Rancid Butter:* Melt and skim the butter. Put into the fat a piece of toast . . .
>
> *How to Clean Playing Cards:* Place them on a newspaper, sprinkle with talcum powder and rub with a piece of clean, dry cheesecloth . . .
>
> *How to Banish Cockroaches:* If cockroaches and ants are troublesome in the house, sprinkle ground rice around their haunts. They eat greedily and it swells inside them and they die.

This obsessive devotion to housework can easily be ridiculed, but to what extent is it still part of an accepted female behavior today? How common is the traditional belief that a woman's place is in the home, that men are to be cooked for, cleaned for, and cared for, first by a mother, then by a wife; that women who do infringe on this code and go out to work have only themselves to blame if their doing so results in broken marriages, drug-addicted children, disintegration of families, and domestic violence?

The socially conservative right-wing British newspaper the *Daily Mail* prints a steady flow of stories undermining women working outside the home:

Nearly nine in ten British women plan to quit their jobs to look after their children, a survey has found. The research flies in the face of the idea that women want to have it all by juggling a career and having children. As well as giving up work, the poll showed that women want large families. One in three said they would have four or more children if money weren't an issue. It provides a revealing insight into women's attitudes to work and relationships and their commitment to family lives. One in five who already have children thought that women who work while raising a family make worse mothers.[4]

Women still do the majority of household tasks, despite participating more in the labor market than in the past. A recent 2007 survey in Britain found that the gendered "chores gap"—for unpaid domestic work at home—is worsening, with working women spending an average of 180 minutes a day on housework, compared to 101 minutes a day for men. The former Equal Opportunities Commission in Britain said that it believes this gap will never close, and that women will continue to spend in excess of 78 percent more time doing housework each day than men.[5]

## Outside the Home: Dress Codes

By staying confined within the home, in the domestic sphere, women are approved of by society at large and perceived to be safe and contained. When women venture outside, their appearance, throughout all cultures and all historical periods, has been a focus of mass observation and censure. For women in the public arena, the amount of flesh on display becomes charged with eroticism. In the West before the twentieth century, showing a few inches above the foot, perhaps an ankle or a glimpse of a calf as a woman moved around, getting in and out of carriages, was seen as highly sexually exciting. In the Indian Subcontinent today, the traditional sari exposes a woman's midriff and back, which isn't considered immodest. However, the sari shirt covers the underarm area, which is seen as erotic and risky to expose, as is showing the leg above the knee.

Different cultures have different dress codes for women—for instance orthodox Jewish women don't show their hair to anyone other than their husbands, and so usually wear a wig or a hat outside the home, and they dress modestly.

Hastings Banda was president of Malawi from 1961 to 1994, and part of his very authoritarian rule included restrictions on women's dress; women were barred from wearing trousers or skirts that ended above the knees. These strictures also applied to female tourists, and border guards stopped women from entering the country in trousers. Women had to wrap a towel around themselves to make an impromptu skirt at the border crossing into Malawi. Hastings Banda's argument for enforcing the dress code—that it instilled respect for women in Malawian society, and particular respect from men—is one often used in different societies to justify taking away freedom of choice from women about what they wear outside the home. He also enforced rules about the length of men's hair, and "hippie" trousers were forbidden.

> Tell the faithful women to lower their gaze and guard their private parts and not display their beauty except what is apparent of it, and to extend their scarf to cover their bosom.
> —Koran, 24:31

The Koran addresses all believers of Islam and asks them to dress modestly, but there has been much highly charged political and private debate on how these injunctions about dress in the public sphere apply to women specifically. There are two traditional ways that Muslim women can cover up—the *hijab,* which is the more common form of headscarf, covering a woman's hair and neck, and the *niqab* (full veil), which covers a woman completely. Of course many Muslim women wear neither the hijab nor the niqab, and their dress codes vary across the Muslim world from Indonesia to Morocco. In the West the "headscarf debate," as it has become known, is a fraught political issue. In western European countries such as France and Britain there have been court battles and intense public debates over whether women and girls should be allowed to wear the headscarf when at school, when meeting their members of parliament, or when teaching primary-school age children. Afsanah Safa, who is British and in her twenties, describes her experiences wearing the hijab:

> " I've been wearing a headscarf since I was twelve years old. When I started wearing it people were a bit surprised because I didn't wear it in the first year of school, then I took it off for a while, then I put it back on so they must have thought what's going on here, but it's OK now. I've been wearing it constantly for the last five years. Wearing a headscarf and covering your body is a way of detracting attention away from yourself. It's a way of preventing men [from] looking at you as a kind of sex object, so they don't have these kind of ideas as you walk down the street, because this is bad for you. We believe that you could get punished for this, if they have these thoughts about you. There are advantages and disadvantages about being brought up in England. You want to be like everyone else, you want to go out and have fun, and sometimes wearing a headscarf restricts these things. You can't go into a bar or a club wearing a headscarf, it's like being a nun or something, it doesn't feel right. When people look at you they must think oh she's very religious, not very interesting, a bit boring, and I really don't like that. I don't want people to look at me and see the headscarf. Wearing the headscarf it's like a constant reminder of who I am. It always reminds me of

> what I'm supposed to do and what I'm not sup-
> posed to do, it's like having your Mum over your
> shoulder telling you what to do. When I don't have
> it on I do feel more free sometimes, I think there's
> nothing holding me back. I do take it off some-
> times, like when we have our school prom, other-
> wise I feel quite awkward. My mum's OK about it,
> on those special occasions, but it doesn't mean I
> go completely crazy, I still remember who I am,
> it's just good to get out of it sometimes.[6]

Many Muslim women remain unveiled and feel no contradiction between this and remaining true to their religion. In Turkey, a majority Muslim but secular state (over 99 percent of the population is Muslim), the headscarf has traditionally been banned in public places, including schools and government institutions. Women wearing headscarves have been refused treatment at state medical facilities. This has polarized society and caused huge controversy, with protests and boycotts of universities by those arguing that by being denied the right to wear a headscarf, many women are de facto being denied the right to higher education and jobs. In February 2008 the Turkish parliament lifted the ban, but four months later the proposed amendment to the constitution was annulled by the country's constitutional court, which cannot be appealed. So the ban is still in place in Turkey, and women's dress—the wearing of a headscarf—has become a political symbol of the state's secularity on the one hand and the fear of a growing Islamization on the other.

Conversely, in Iran and Saudi Arabia, women are forced to follow a strict Islamic dress code, wearing the *hijab* and *abaya* (a long black cloak) outside the home. Religious police are there to enforce the law, and women who don't cover up are punished.

## Asking for It

Descriptions of sexual violence and attacks on women are often subtly connected to how the women were dressed at the time, as a way of diverting blame and distracting the jury from what really went on. If a rape victim is reported as wearing a short skirt, high heels, or a revealing top, she is portrayed in the media and sometimes by the judicial system as having somehow provoked the attack, of having "asked for it."

In the impoverished French ghettoes in cities such as Paris, Marseille, Lyons, or Toulouse, there have been incidents of gang rapes and violence by Muslim men and boys targeting those women and girls in their community who they consider to be dressing in a manner that is too "Western." Samira Bellil, a famous French Muslim activist who died in 2004, was raped at the age of thirteen, and brought this systematic violence into the public eye by talking about it openly when another thirteen-year-old girl in Lille, who was raped by eighty men, brought her attackers to trial. Bellil was close to the organization called Ni Putes, Ni Soumises, (Neither whores nor doormats [submissives]) set up in 2003 by a group of young French

Muslim women to counter this vicious spate of attacks against women perceived to be breaking dress codes outside the home.[7]

Women all over the world, whether or not they abide by traditional dress codes, are always conscious of the reaction they get from the men who pass them on the street and in public places. It's rare that they can move around freely outside the home unless they are older, post-menopausal, "invisible" to society, and therefore not interesting to men—and then they are often ignored in public places, and can find it hard to get attention from men or women.

## Education for All

*If women are expected to do the same work as men, we must teach them the same things.*

—Plato, 427–347 BC

*The Intellectual Inferiority of Women*
*Death from Overstudy*

—newspaper headlines[8]

Only in the twentieth century did women's education start to become recognized as a universal right, if not a reality, for many millions of girls and women throughout the world. The prevailing view before that had been that educating women was a dangerous activity. It would result in chaos at home with women abandoning their domestic roles as housekeepers and child minders. Mothers were warned that their university-educated "bluestocking" daughters would be unmarriageable, and the press ridiculed women's attempts to get into universities or places of higher education.

## Graduating Women

Oxford University is the oldest university in the English-speaking world, founded in the twelfth century. For the first 800 years of its existence, no women were allowed to study there. Only in 1878 were two colleges established for women, but these first students were not allowed to become full members of the university; women could only begin graduating with Oxford degrees in 1920. Without a university degree, it was very difficult for women to enter the professions, and by 1900 there were still only 200 women doctors in the United Kingdom. In 1910 women were allowed to become accountants and bankers, but there were still no female diplomats, barristers, or judges. In the United States, universities were opened up to women earlier, and women's colleges were established. In 1837 Oberlin College in Ohio began granting degrees to women, becoming the first coeducational institution of higher learning in the United States; in 1862 the college saw the graduation of Mary Jane Patterson, the first African-American woman to receive a bachelor's degree. That Patterson managed this in the face of the prevailing opinion of women and racism at the time is even more impressive.

Henry James was an author who created some of the most lively, enduring, and compelling female heroines—women like Isabel Archer in *Portrait of a Lady* or Charlotte Stant in *The Golden Bowl*. Yet in the mid-nineteenth century he could still write:

> Learning and wisdom do not become her . . . women's true nature is not to promote the spread of science and art, is not to do battle with ignorance and superstition, is not to wrest the great field of nature from the domination of savage beast; it is simply to refine and enervate man.
>
> —Henry James, "Women and
> the Women Question,"
> *Putnam's Monthly* 1 (March 1853)

Over sixty years earlier, the London-born writer and freethinking feminist Mary Wollstonecraft had pleaded for equality in male and female education in her treatise *A Vindication of the Rights of Woman*. She said that keeping women in their current state of ignorance was a degradation of her sex, and that, without education, women are debased and cannot hope to escape from male domination, and would therefore always remain inferior to men.

> [W]omen must be allowed to found their virtue on knowledge, which is scarcely possible unless they be educated by the same pursuits as men. For they are now made so inferior by ignorance and low desires, as not to deserved to

> be ranked with them . . . It is plain from the history of all nations, that women cannot be confined to merely domestic pursuits, for they will not fulfill family duties, unless their minds take a wider range, and whilst they are kept in ignorance they become in the same proportion the slaves of pleasure as they are the slaves of men.[9]

## Education and Development

Education is a way of making sure that girls and boys have the same start in life and the chance to grow and develop according to their potential. This means that all girls and boys are to have an equal opportunity to enjoy a high-quality basic education. In 1990 the Education for All movement was launched at a UNESCO World Conference. It's aim is to achieve gender equality in education by 2015.

The benefits of female education go far beyond the individual. Educated mothers are far more likely to send their own daughters to school, to better look after the health of their families, and to have smaller families. Educated women are less exposed to sexual exploitation and health risks such as HIV and AIDS infection.[10] In South Asia, 66 percent of all unschooled children are girls. In Afghanistan, 87 percent of women are illiterate, and only 30 percent of girls have access to any education.[11] So there is a long way to go, and until education is freely available for both sexes, societies have scant chance of being changed from within. Without education, women can do very little in the public space.[12]

## What's Stopping Girls from Learning?

At the beginning of the twenty-first century, many factors prevent girls around the world from attending school. State-sponsored public education is not available in many places, and high school fees prevent many poor families from educating their daughters. Even where there is some form of free public education, there may also be the expenses of paying for a uniform, books, and transportation. When there is a choice to be made, families often send their sons rather than their daughters to school, placing a premium on educating the perceived future earner and head of the household. Many schools, especially in rural areas of developing countries, are also unwelcome environments for girls. A lack of separate bathroom facilities, sexual harassment, and discrimination deter parents from sending their daughters. Coupled with that is the distance involved in getting to school in some remote places. Parents may fear the girls will be vulnerable on the journey, being at risk of sexual attack, or, alternatively, that they may mix with boys and bring dishonor on the family whether or not they have sex.

Girls in the developing world often have to take on heavy domestic duties from an early age, particularly if they belong to big households or if their mothers are ill or dead. This stops them from going to school or forces them to drop out prematurely. Early or child marriage also puts a stop to a girl's education, making it far harder for her to find a job later on and to manage her family and sexual relationships because she will be entirely dependent on her husband, or another male. In Ethiopia, for example, around 80 percent of young married women have had no education and are unable to read.[13]

Educating all children equally by avoiding prejudices and sexist stereotypes is the most valuable tool available to any society. Until this has been achieved, however, girls' and women's education around the world is still at risk.

But the battle is not all in the developing world; there are cases of prejudice against educated women in the United States. In 2006 the editor of *Forbes* magazine, Michael Noer, argued in an article published in his magazine that college-educated women with careers are more likely to be dissatisfied with their husbands, have extramarital sex, neglect housekeeping, and possibly even earn more than their husbands—all of which, he says, makes for rocky marriages.

> " Guys: A word of advice. Marry pretty women or ugly ones. Short ones or tall ones. Blondes or brunettes. Just, whatever you do, don't marry a woman with a career.[14]

Noer's words caused a huge controversy, and the editor in chief of *Forbes* swiftly issued a public apology. Yet attitudes like Michael Noer's also exist in the right-wing British press, which publishes numerous articles on the unhappy lot of educated career women. This is typical:

> On the face of it, women have gained much over the last few decades—careers, greater independence and a chance to make an impact on the world . . . But as their choices and opportunities have increased, their happiness seems to have diminished, according to a survey.
>
> The first study was the work of husband and wife economists Betsey Stevenson and Justin Wolfers at the University of Pennsylvania. They said that in 1976, 16 percent of men were satisfied with their lives. This has increased to 25 percent today, according to their survey. But the number of women who are happy has stayed at 22 percent. Miss Stevenson said: "Thirty or forty years ago, women were happier because they probably had narrower ambitions. They compared themselves to each other and not to men. Now women are more competitive and more ambitious. But it seems it doesn't make them any happier."[15]

## Public Space: Women outside the Home

*Recalling that I recognize in women a natural talent for dominating men, many readers—I imagine—will accuse me of contradicting myself; yet they will be mistaken. There is an important difference between usurping the right to command and governing the one who commands.*

*Woman's empire is one of sweetness, artfulness, and an ac-commodating spirit. Her orders come as caresses, her threats as tears. She should rule her household like a min-ister his government, by having herself ordered to do what she wishes . . . But when she fails to heed the voice of the true head of the family and tries to usurp his rights and to command alone, this disorder leads to nothing but mis-ery, scandal and dishonour.*

Jean-Jacques Rousseau,
*Le Contrat Social* IV 1762

## Resentment—Stealing Men's Jobs

During World War I and World War II, women took over many men's jobs. There was an active public campaign to get women into munitions factories and onto the land, driving tractors, to fill the roles vacated by men who had left to fight in the wars. Women largely relished this op-portunity to get out of the home, to enter the public space, to feel useful and valued, and to have new and challeng-ing responsibilities outside the home. After the war, with the return of the demobilized soldiers, women were told to give up their jobs to the men and to get themselves back into the home.

Historians have argued that this taste of freedom and the satisfaction of useful employment in the public space opened a window of opportunity for women, who were reluctant to relinquish it afterward. The women who worked during the war discovered that there was no mystique about male-dominated employment. They didn't want to be forced back into the domestic sphere and have the door kicked shut behind them again for good.

*A riveter at Lockheed Aircraft Corporation in Burbank, California during World War II. Photo courtesy of the National Archives and Records Administration.*

Working outside the Home

To paraphrase Rousseau and others who still agree with him, a woman's place is in the home, and in that home she should bow to her husband's moral and intellectual authority. So women's power and authority has tradition- ally and culturally been constricted into a narrow physical space and emotional sphere of influence. Keeping house, bearing and rearing children, being economically de- pendent on their husbands and fathers—women's activi- ties are sanctioned within the sacred domestic space of their home. However, when they do venture out to try to gain economic independence, to compete with men in the workplace, to write, comment, or take on political power, the assumption is often that these women are fair game.

Sometimes women have no choice but to enter the public space, when conflict or the death of their partners changes the situation. This has been the case for a number of Palestinian women in the last few years:

> With tighter restrictions on the movement of men, many women are forced out of their pro- tected domestic cocoons to seek employment to sustain their families, while their unemployed husbands stay at home. This sudden and invol- untary reversal of gender roles disturbs the sta- bility of intra-family relationships, and puts women in a perilous position. Many men resort to violent means to assert their control over the family, feeling insecure about their status in the family, and frustrated by feelings of helplessness

> and powerlessness. Not surprisingly, male frustration and insecurity have a consequent adverse impact on women, who become victims of increased rates of domestic violence.[16]

## Murders in Guatemala

Nearly 2,000 Guatemalan women were tortured and killed between 2001 and 2006. Police say numbers are still rising, as is the rate of sexual violence toward women. The vast majority of these murders remain uninvestigated and unpunished; Guatemalan activists see them as a vicious backlash against women taking up paid work alongside men, being out on the streets, away from the domestic scene. One case was that of the nineteen-year-old law student Claudina Isabel Velázquez Paíz, who was traveling between her home and the university in Guatemala City when she disappeared. The following day her body was found; there were traces of semen on her clothes, and she had been shot in the head. Like the other murders of women in Guatemala, activists say the police failed to follow leads, no forensic tests were carried out on her clothes, and potential witnesses were not pursued.[17] Her father still fights for justice:

> Claudina was killed by one thing: impunity . . . Claudina's killer knew that the likelihood of him being found was very remote . . . The investigator said they thought Claudina was a nobody because she was wearing sandals and a belly button ring.[18]

## Public Women Who Pay the Price

*"I get into the vehicle and think that somewhere along the route, in the dark . . . I am obviously going to be killed."*[19]

*Memorial gathering for Anna Politkovskaya in Tokyo. Photo courtesy of Amnesty International.*

This is what the Russian political activist and journalist Anna Politkovskaya wrote in her diary as she returned from a meeting with Ramzan Kadyrov, the man who in 2007 became president of Chechnya. In fact, Anna Politkovskaya wasn't killed on her way back to Grozny, but on the steps of her apartment building in Moscow, where she was brutally gunned down on October 7, 2006.

Of course male journalists are murdered for their work as well, especially while covering the war in Iraq, but in the case of women there is often a subtle, or not-so-subtle, inference in the media that these women shouldn't have been where they were in the first place, and that they have only themselves to blame. If they have children—like Anna Politkovskaya and the Irish investigative journalist Veronica Guerin, who was shot dead by drug dealers in 1996—the undercurrent of opinion is that they were irresponsible to have put themselves at risk and leave their children motherless.

The explorer Alison Hargreaves, the first British woman to climb Mount Everest unsupported by oxygen or sherpas, died on a subsequent expedition to K2 in 1995, leaving behind her husband, Jim Ballard, and two children, then aged six and four. This is what her husband recalls about the immediate aftermath of her death:

> There were some very hurtful things said in the press after Alison died. The charge that she was irresponsible for leaving her children was the least of them. I had a very sticky time defending the right of women to do the kind of things

> Alison did, but, at the same time, enormous numbers of people wrote to me to say it helped them to climb the mountains of everyday life.[20]

Living with Fear

The Yemeni journalist Huda Al-Attas has written an article calling for women to unveil in public in her society, and for that she was condemned by the religious authorities. She has been put on a death list by extreme Islamic fundamentalists:

> So many nights, I stayed up thinking that tomorrow I could be killed. I know my phone calls are being tapped and even when I talk to my husband, I become curt and dry, knowing there's a third ear listening to our most private conversations.[21]

Huda Al-Attas says that her determination to speak out and act in the public arena came from her mother's encouragement and protection. She had prevented Huda from being married off at the age of twelve:

> My father was adamant on getting me married, but my mother would have nothing of it and encouraged me to continue my education. She even bought me a bicycle and when the woman next door disapproved, saying that I would lose my virginity due to riding it, my mother bought me a bigger, prettier one! It was then that I

" knew I was different and would have to challenge my way to freedom.[22]

The message for all women from Huda's story is that parents, and especially mothers, are crucial in giving their daughters confidence to enter the public space, to lead by example, and to claim their right to be seen and heard outside the home.

## Virtual Slavery

*As a domestic worker, you have no control over your life. No one respects you. You have no rights. This is the lowest kind of work.*

> —Hasana, child domestic worker who began
> working when she was twelve years old,
> Jogjakarta, Indonesia, 2004

*If I did something the employer didn't like, she would grab my hair and hit my head on the wall. She would say things like, "I don't pay you to sit and watch TV! You don't wash the dishes well. I pay your mother good money and you don't do anything [to deserve it]." . . . Once I forgot clothes in the washer, and they started to smell, so she grabbed my head and tried to stick it in the washing machine.*

> —Saida B, child domestic worker, aged fifteen,
> Casablanca, Morocco, 2005

*I was locked up inside the agency for 45 days. We were Indonesians and Filipinas; 25 of us. We got food only once*

*a day. We couldn't go out at all. The agency said we owed
them 1,500 Dhm—three months' salary. Five of us ran
away; we used a blanket to escape from the second floor.
Four of us got injured.*

—Cristina Suarez, Filipina domestic worker,
age twenty-six, Dubai, United Arab Emirates,
February 27, 2006

*When the lady went to drop off the children to the grand-
mother's house, the man would stay at home . . . he raped
me many, many times; once a day, every day for three
months. He hit me a lot because I didn't want to have sex.
I don't know what a condom is, but he used some tissues
after he raped me.*

—Zakiah, returned domestic worker from Malaysia,
age twenty, January 24, 2004[23]

## The Invisible Labor Force

Half of the 200 million migrants worldwide are women,
working predominantly as foreign domestic workers. This
wave of women leaving their homes to find work as house-
maids and child carers, many in the Middle East and Asia,
is particularly pronounced in the Philippines, Sri Lanka,
and Indonesia, where women make up 60–75 percent of
legal migrants from their countries of origin. The money
they send back to their families is a valuable source of foreign revenue for the country, yet these women are often
left legally unprotected as domestic workers, both in their

home countries and in the places where they're working. They can be stranded in exploitative working conditions very far away from home. There are hidden penalties in ignoring these women. For instance, Sri Lanka currently has a very low HIV/AIDS infection rate (under 1,000 reported cases in a population of 19 million in 2007[24]) compared to its South Asian neighbors, particularly India, but very unusually, more women than men are infected there. HIV/AIDS campaigners in Sri Lanka say this has happened because women domestic workers contract the virus in the Persian Gulf or wherever they are working abroad, often through being sexually abused by their employers. When they come home, their husbands are put at risk. Many of these women are Tamils from the tea estates, the poorest and most dispossessed people in Sri Lanka. Thousands of mothers leave their children behind to work overseas, and the terrible side effects of their absence are increased rates of incest in the families, and husbands who drink or squander much of the money sent home by their wives—money that is intended for building a house or educating the children. Sometimes these women return after absences of five years or more to find nothing to show for all the hard-earned money they have sent home.

### Working in the Gulf
Domestic workers in the Gulf Cooperation Council (Bahrain, Kuwait, Oman, Qatar, Saudi Arabia, and the United Arab Emirates) have no legal protection. They face

discriminatory laws; in particular they are excluded from equality and labor laws. They are often not given access to legal advice or interpreters, and they find the process of trying to get justice overwhelmingly intimidating.

Two women, one from India, the other from Indonesia, were each sentenced to one year's imprisonment and 100 lashes in Ras al-Khaimah Emirate, the United Arab Emirates (UAE), for becoming pregnant outside marriage. The men responsible for their pregnancies were not arrested or charged with any offence.[25]

In February 2005 the Saudi Arabian Minister of Labor started a process to ban more than 1,000 employers from employing migrant workers—acknowledging that abuses have gone on. It is still unclear whether female domestic workers would be included in any new labor protection scheme for migrant workers.

### No Protection at All

Nepali women working in the Gulf are particularly vulnerable because they are working there illegally. In 1998 the Nepalese government banned all women from domestic work abroad after a woman was allegedly killed by her employer in Saudi Arabia. Despite this, women continue to leave Nepal each week, desperate to find work abroad, but, due to the lack of any bilateral agreement between Nepal and the countries they work in, these women are particularly vulnerable to being underpaid and sexually exploited. Each year, Nepal's migrant workers send back over 1 billion dollars of their wages. About 10 percent of this comes from illegal domestic workers who pay too high a price for the foreign revenue the country enjoys.

As Sharu Joshi of the United Nations Development Fund for Women (UNIFEM) says, "Despite their huge contribution, the [Nepali] government is doing nothing to protect them or introduce laws in favour of these poor migrant female workers."

## Modern-day Slavery in Britain

The famous case of Mende Nazer directed a spotlight onto the problem of slavery in Britain. She says she was abducted and sold into slavery as a young girl in Sudan, eventually ending up working as a slave in London. In 2002 she escaped and applied for asylum, which was initially refused. Human rights groups, including Anti-Slavery International, took up her case, and the Home Office (the U.K. government department responsible for immigration control, security, and order) later supported her plea for asylum, not on the grounds of slavery, but rather because she was so well known, and her case was so highly publicized that her life might have been in jeopardy back in Sudan.

> Now I feel I'm free because I am doing things I never used to do before . . . For me the reason for talking out is to help make another slave free—not just a slave from Sudan, but from anywhere in the world. By talking out, people will be more aware and more able to help people become free.[26]

## Female Child Labor

Exploitative working conditions often make domestic labor one of the worst forms of child labor. Hidden inside a home, these children have no rights and are at the mercy of their employers. The International Labour Organization (ILO) estimates that more girls under sixteen work in domestic service than in any other category of child labor. For example, the ILO believes that there are nearly 700,000 child domestic workers in Indonesia, and that 20,000 girls and women between the ages of fourteen and nineteen are in this situation in El Salvador.[27]

In 2007 a survey indicated that thirty-two out of thirty-three of the London boroughs estimated they had a child trafficking problem; the boroughs reported that children were being used for domestic labor, in the catering industry, and in the sex industry.[28]

## Domestic Workers in Latin America

> It is very probable that if a domestic worker begins to talk about rights she will be fired.
>
> —Emilio Alvarez Icaza, president of the
> Human Rights Commission in Mexico

In Latin America, millions of women are domestic workers. It is estimated that 15 percent of the female workforce there is employed in an industry that has been described as legalized discrimination and even modern-day slavery.[29]

But a breakthrough occurred in Bolivia in 2006 when Casimira Rodriguez, a Quechua Indian woman who was a former domestic worker, became minister for justice. At the age of thirteen, Rodriguez had been taken from her village in the Andes and forced to work as a servant for fifteen people. Her servitude lasted eighteen years. Being exploited, she says, gave her the will to challenge the status of domestic workers, and her aim as cabinet minister was to reform corruption and inefficiency, particularly in the judicial system.

## Sticky Floors

*Women are not inherently passive or peaceful. We're not inherently anything but human.*

—Robin Morgan, U.S. civil rights activist
and feminist writer

*I've always felt that a woman's style of leadership doesn't have to be an imitation of a masculine style. I think masculine leadership is often very competitive, very aggressive, and I never felt that my own style which was people-orientated, compassionate, intelligent, was in any way inferior to men's style of leadership.*

General Eva Burrows, the first woman
to be elected General of the
Salvation Army, 1986–1993[30]

Women in the Workforce

Women take on two-thirds of the world's work but earn only one-tenth of its income. Seventy percent of the 1.2 billion people living in poverty throughout the world are women. Women's relative lack of education compared to men and the demands of bearing and raising children mean that their access to work outside the home is severely curtailed.

When women do enter the workforce, there are hidden barriers and subtle forms of lingering prejudice waiting for them.

> The worst advice I ever got was "Stick with me, babe." And it usually came from a male mentor who treated me like a jewel locked away in a closet. I could always feel the imprint of his foot as he stepped on my back to climb that ladder. This happens to women all the time when they think they're being helped. My advice: Seek out mentors that are motivated by *your* best interests, not theirs.
>
> —Kathy Biro, cofounder and vice chair of the U.S. marketing and technology firm Digitas

### *Labor and Gendered Wages*
In Britain, despite thirty years of equal pay law, women still earn less than men. Women predominate in part-time work and they earn 39 percent less per hour proportionally

than men in full-time work. The former Equal Opportunities Commission in Britain published a survey in 2007 showing that five years after leaving university, women were earning 15 percent less than men. This gender pay gap exists even when women have studied the same subject, earned the same degree as men, and work in the same occupation or industry as them.[31]

Research by an economist at Carnegie Mellon University in the United States has found an interesting angle to this gendered pay gap among working women. It showed that men were better both at negotiating higher starting salaries and pushing for pay rises throughout their careers. When students with a master's degree who had received job offers were asked whether they had accepted the starting salary they were offered, 51 percent of the men said no, that they had pushed for more. But when women with master's degrees were asked the same question, only 12.5 percent said they had negotiated upward—that's four times fewer women than men.[32] So is the answer to train women to be more aggressive, to not take no for an answer? Perhaps it's not quite so straightforward. Another study done in 2007 again coming out of the United States, this time from Harvard, shows that men and women get different reactions when they try to bargain. Women are thought of as "less nice" when they push for more money, and they are perceived negatively by both men and women on interview panels. Men negotiating for a raise are not penalized in the same way. Hannah Riley Bowles carried out the experiments:

> " What we found across all the studies is that men were always less willing to work with a woman who had attempted to negotiate than with a woman who did not . . . They always preferred to work with a woman who stayed mum. But it made no difference to the men whether a guy had chosen to negotiate.[33]

So the situation is complex: there are higher risks for women pushing for a better deal, and, as it turns out, female candidates are responding accurately to how they will be perceived by their seniors. "This isn't about fixing the women," says Hannah Riley Bowles.[34]

### Glass Ceilings

Glass ceilings and sticky floors are both analogies of women's careers—stuck in low- and mid-level positions, they get so far and then no farther. The International Federation of Journalists found that although nearly one-third of journalists today are women, only 3 percent are in senior management positions in media organizations. In the academic world, while an increasing number of women are graduating from universities—often with better grades than men—still relatively very few are becoming academics or university chancellors and presidents. Women don't find it as easy to get the same funding for research as their male counterparts. Even among nongovernmental organizations (NGOs), where women have found empowerment and a strong political voice, far fewer of the female employees get to decision-making levels than do men.[35]

## Women in the Boardroom

In 2009, there were only five female CEOs in the top 100 group of companies listed on the London stock exchange. Throughout the United Kingdom, less than a quarter of all directors of businesses are women, and those who are usually run smaller and medium-sized organizations in education, health, social work, hospitality, and leisure sectors. This pattern is similar in Australia, where women represent 43 percent of the total workforce, but only 3.2 percent of the top executives are female.[36] The picture is not much better in the United States, where in the first decade of the twenty-first century, the percentage of women at executive level in the top 500 companies doubled to just over 16 percent. At this rate it will take forty years for gender equality to be achieved.[37]

But what about those women who do break through to compete in a man's world?

Yve Newbold, who was the company secretary of a large Anglo-American conglomerate, says,

> It's often the very small, minor pricks of life that add up to a lot of stress and pressure over a working lifetime. We women probably feel like pioneers, and pioneers always have a hard time, but I hope we're making it easier for those coming behind us. Also, what I call the drawbridge mentality, when women think "Well, I got here by myself, therefore you can" is a strange one, and therefore I love, wherever I can, to give a helping hand to women coming up.[38]

Apart from the barriers men put up to stop women from getting into the boardroom, there is also research which says that women themselves have an "inner inhibitor" to this kind of success. They decide it comes at too high a personal price. For women to have an advantage equal to that of men, the culture of business and the boardroom needs to change. The macho image of working long hours, sacrificing family and a social life, and being driven only by work still prevails, and while it does, women are often not prepared or are unable to make that kind of sacrifice.

Trevor Phillips, head of the Commission for Equality and Human Rights in the United Kingdom, says that Britain is currently wasting a potential £20 billion worth of productivity because women are unable to access the job market in a way that fits in with the rest of their lives and responsibilities:

> It's dumb . . . we need all the clever women we've got whether they've got children or not . . . We can't just make some concessions so women can do jobs in the way men do them, we have to change the whole way we work.[39]

He wants companies to let women work whenever they want and take time off whenever they want, to forget about a traditional eight-hour, five-day work week and introduce something different, like "annualized" hours that women could make up over a year, working when it suits them.

## *The Glass Cliff*

For those women who do break through and get to the top of their professions, they come up against another hurdle called the glass cliff. Women find it very hard to land senior jobs; as a result, they have no choice but to accept leadership positions that are very risky. They are often offered the top jobs at failing companies because the firm is desperate. Women take on these difficult roles, jobs that few men in equivalent positions would consider, and that may well turn out to be career suicide, because the options open to them at that level are severely limited.

It is often said that a woman must work twice as hard as a man to get to an equivalent position of responsibility. Coupled with that, she will often be managing the domestic life of her family as well. But the status quo isn't going to shift until enough women do get to positions of power to sway the balance in the boardroom and, little by little, change our notions of what it means to be in business for either men or women.

## Women Out There in Space

Some bastions of male territory are being broken down very convincingly and without stet big fanfare. In October 2007, history was made 220 miles above the Earth. On arrival, when pilot Pamela Melroy docked the U.S. space shuttle Discovery onto the International Space Station, the hatches were opened and she embraced Peggy Whitson, the commander of the station. This was a far cry from what happened in 1961, when a group of women pilots

who took the same tests and training as the male astro-
nauts were never allowed to fly. Pamela Melroy made a
telling point about this historic meeting—pointing out
that for once this wasn't gender tokenism or a stage-man-
aged photo opportunity: "This happened by accident. Nobody said 'Hey, wouldn't it be neat if we could have this or
this?' That is the ultimate goal, when you get to a point
where nobody thinks twice about this stuff."[40]

## Half the Sky

*Women hold up half the sky.*

—Chinese proverb

*When Ben Gurion is reputed to have said that she was
the best man he had in the cabinet, she replied "Yes, but
why do you think it is a compliment to be the best man?"
When she was asked "How do you feel like being the first
woman prime minister?" she replied, "I don't know, I've
never tried being a man prime minister."*

—Simcha Dinitz, political advisor to Golda Meir,
Israeli prime minister, 1969–1973.[41]

### Women in Power

There are around 7,500 women currently holding political office in the world, as opposed to nearly 36,000 men.
That's only one in five, when women make up over half of
the total population.[42] Scandinavia and Rwanda have the
best record—over half of their politicians are women. The

Arab States have the worst record with 8.8 percent women politicians. Why are there proportionately so few women politicians? Some might say these statistics aren't bad considering that women only received the right to vote within the last hundred years—but it's also the usual combination of lack of education, heavy domestic responsibilities, financial dependence, and negative cultural attitudes toward women taking up such a very public space that have impeded and sometimes blocked women from assuming an equal share of political power.

### Taking Power

> *I was elected not as a woman, but as a human being . . .*
> *Afterward, I realized how fine it was for my country that*
> *this had happened. I was proud of my countrymen to have*
> *the guts to do that.*

Vigdís Finnbogadóttir was president of Iceland from 1980 to 1996. She was the world's first elected female president, despite being a divorced single mother. Iceland achieved another first in February 2009, electing the world's first openly lesbian prime minister, Johanna Sigurdadottir.

The last fifty years have seen the rise of women to the highest political office—there have been nearly fifty female presidents or prime ministers since Srimavo Bandaranaike became the world's first woman prime minister in 1960 in Ceylon (later renamed Sri Lanka). She succeeded her husband, Solomon Bandaranaike, who had been assassinated the year before and started the South Asian trend of dynastic political families that often led to a woman in power after the death of a male relative—Indira Gandhi of India, Benazir Bhutto of Pakistan (the first female head of an Islamic country), Khaleda Zia of Bangladesh, and Aung San Suu Kyi, who was democratically elected to lead Burma in 1990 with a landslide victory of 82 percent. Suu Kyi's election was nullified in a coup, and she has lived under house arrest ever since, with the country ruled by a military junta.

> " Especially in post-conflict situations, where new constitutions and legislative structures are being created, it is critical that women are present at the peace table and in post-war policy-making.
> —UN Development Fund for Women (UNIFEM), former Executive Director Noeleen Heyzer (1994–2007)[43]

Some countries have taken advantage of a postconflict situation to promote more women in parliament. In Rwanda, after the 1994 genocide, women's groups lobbied hard for better representation and they achieved the best proportion of women in parliament anywhere in the world.[44] Women seized the opportunity to carve out a political future for themselves by making sure they were there at the right time. The Rwandan constitution makes it mandatory for a third of the cabinet to be women. Women currently hold the foreign, education, and information portfolios; the head of the supreme court and the police are women, as are the holders of forty-five of the eighty parliamentary seats.

Ellen Johnson-Sirleaf, who was elected president of Liberia in 2005, is both that country's and Africa's first woman head of state. She, like Portia Simpson Miller, Jamaica's prime minister from 2006 to 2007, is taking up the most difficult political challenges of the twenty-first century—leadership in countries riven by poverty and violence.

Representation of women at the very top doesn't come without penalties. Malalai Joya, the youngest member of parliament in Afghanistan and a women's activist, isn't afraid to speak out against the warlords, but she's also received death threats and has already survived four assassination attempts. She says there is a price on her head, and she never sleeps in the same place twice. Ironically, the burqa she wears in public is also the perfect disguise to hide her from her enemies.[45] Malalai Joya was suspended from parliament in May 2007 for giving an interview to a private Afghan television channel in which she described the parliament as being worse than a stable of animals.

### Women and Surrogate Power

There were also plenty of women in the twentieth century who wielded influence behind their powerful husbands— Elena Ceaucescu of Romania; Jiang Ching, better known as Madam Mao in China; Imelda Marcos of the Philippines; Nancy Reagan and Hillary Clinton as first ladies in the United States; and today the world scrutinizes First Lady Michelle Obama's influence on her husband. The public debate surrounding these women generally casts them as the evil and sinister partners of their husbands. Some were portrayed as equally, if not more, cruel and sadistic than the men, and they were also particularly censured and vilified for their so-called feminine traits of acquisitiveness and rapaciousness—often criticized for their shopping habits, their materialism, their obsessions with clothes, jewels, and shoes.

Margaret Thatcher, Britain's first woman prime minister (1979–1990), and the leader who has arguably had the biggest impact on British politics and society since World War II, was portrayed as a sexual dominatrix or a harridan in satirical cartoons at the time. The phrase "to handbag" came from the image of Margaret Thatcher hitting her colleagues over the head with a large black handbag to quell them into submission. *Spitting Image,* the satirical puppet show that ran on British television from 1984 to 1996, had a notorious sketch of Mrs. Thatcher in a restaurant, sitting at the top of the table, surrounded by her all-male cabinet. The waiter takes her order: "Steak, I'll have the steak," she says. "And how would madam like it?" "Raw!" says Mrs. Thatcher. "And what about the vegetables, Madam?" to which she responds, "They'll have the same as me."

### Into Battle

*I know I have the body of a weak and feeble woman, but I have the heart and stomach of a king, and of a king of England too; and think foul scorn that Parma or Spain, or any prince of Europe, should dare to invade the borders of my realm.*

—Elizabeth I's famous speech to the
troops at Tilbury on the approach
of the Spanish Armada, 1588

Throughout history, female warrior queens have fought and led their troops into battle: the Amazons, Queen Artemisia of Persia, Boudicca of the Iceni tribe in ancient Britain, Cleopatra of Egypt, or the Trung sisters, who drove the Chinese out of Vietnam in A.D. 40. Yet the myth still perpetuates that women don't have the guts for the battlefield.

In 1982 Margaret Thatcher took Britain to war against Argentina over the Falkland Islands. Nine years earlier, Israel's prime minister, Golda Meir, responded to Egypt and Syria's attack on the Golan Heights with what became known as the Yom Kippur War. When she was elected prime minister in 1969, Golda Meir had indicated her determination to fight if she had to: "We do not want to be shot at, and believe me we do not want to shoot, but we want borders that we know that, God forbid, if something happens in the future, we know we can defend ourselves."

## The Exclusion Zone

The women who have led their countries form a tiny and select group. The vast majority of the world's leaders have been and still are men. It's not only at governmental level that men predominate; women across the world are excluded from political bodies and left out of the decision-making process. One of the resolutions from the 1995 Beijing Conference on Women underlines how vital it is for women to take political power to make more equal societies:

> Equality in political decision-making performs a leverage function without which it is highly unlikely that a real integration of the equality dimension in government policy-making is feasible. In this respect, women's equal participation in political life plays a pivotal role in the general process of the advancement of women.

*Painting of Joan of Arc by Jules Lenepveu, (1819–1898).*

# 2

# Wives and Daughters

This section looks at the role of women in the domestic sphere, primarily in relation to men, and the ways in which it conditions the choices and opportunities open to them all over the world. It is trite but also true to say that all women are the daughters—and often wives—of men, and that fact generally determines how they are treated. In other words, women's place in society is nearly always second-hand, dependent on their male relatives or spouses. This and the following chapters examine what men's ownership of and power over women means in practical terms, and what happens when women breach conventions and try to carve out independent roles for themselves.

## I Do: Women and Marriage

*I got married because I realised a woman's lot was not all well in Pakistan. I got married because I wanted a house of my own, and single women in Pakistan with good reputations don't live in homes of their own. So you can say that in a way I got married because the realities of the Eastern culture descended on me, and I realised that if I did not marry, I would not be able to pursue my political life. Why? Because my brother got married, and that meant that when he got married, in my own home I would have to ask: "Can I invite guests to dinner?" "Can I use the room to have a committee meeting of the Pakistan People's Party?" I couldn't do that, so then I decided I'm going to get married.*

—Benazir Bhutto, prime minister of
Pakistan 1988–1990, married
Asif Ali Zardari in 1987.
She was the first Muslim woman
to lead her country and the first
woman to give birth while in office.
She was assassinated in a suicide
attack at an election rally in Rawalpindi
in Pakistan on December 27, 2007.[1]

Marriage has always been a social and financial institution as well as a religious one—a way of joining families, retaining property, and expanding empires. Daughters act as commodities; their beauty and desirability are pawns in the game of brokering advantageous financial and property deals. Whether it's the father paying a dowry to his daughter's future in-laws or men paying in cash or goods to secure their future wives, money generally changes hands and, symbolically, women are a property to be exchanged and bartered over.

The history of the Western romance novel is about the conflict between true love and the game of marriage, often with the comic side-plot of an ugly and undesirable daughter to get rid of first. In the traditional Christian marriage service, the woman is handed over to her husband by her father, symbolizing the transfer of ownership of property. In the marriage vows themselves, a woman historically promised to "love, honor, and obey" her new husband as she did her father. For a bride to say "obey" in her marriage service is now unusual; when Sarah Ferguson married Prince Andrew in 1986, she promised to obey him, a pledge Princess Diana omitted from her vows to Prince Charles in 1981. In the Jewish wedding service the Ketubah (marriage contract) is read out loud and the man has to accept the marital responsibility of protecting his wife, giving her clothing, warmth, and shelter, and providing for her after his death or divorce. There is no equivalent contract for the woman's obligation to her husband.

> " Thy husband is thy lord, thy life, thy keeper,
> Thy head, thy sovereign, one that cares for
>     thee,
> And for thy maintenance commits his body
> To painful labour both by sea and land,
> To watch the night in storms, the day in cold,
> Whilst thou liest warm at home, secure and
>     safe,

> And craves no other tribute at thy hands
> But love, fair looks, and true obedience.
> —Kate, after Petruchio has tamed her
> in *The Taming of the Shrew*[2]

For women around the world, marriage is often essential to enable them to act in society—the position of spinster is precarious at best in many cultures. Status, economic power, and sheer survival is dependent on marriage; without it women are often marginalized in their communities, or vilified as being "other": prostitutes, lesbians, or witches.

## I Want You to Meet This Nice Boy/Girl

Arranged marriages, agreed on by two families, are common in many different cultures and religions. In an arranged marriage, the prospective bride and groom may be introduced to each other by a third party, but the final decision whether or not to marry is meant to be their choice. There are hundreds of websites, advertisements, and pages in Indian newspapers and all round the rest of the Subcontinent that are devoted to the personal details—including horoscopes and physical descriptions—of men and women looking for marriage. In Indian law, a dowry can be given but not asked for. Providing dowries for daughters can be a huge financial burden for both the immediate and extended family. In some areas, female infanticide is blamed on the dowry system, with families reluctant to bring up, educate, and feed daughters for whom large amounts of money will eventually have to be found, or to face the stigma and expense of having unmarried daughters at home instead. Selective abortion is illegal, but difficult to prove. Those who die are called the "missing millions"; they have been killed or never allowed to live because they were the wrong sex. There are 60 million "missing" girls and women worldwide.

China's one-child policy was instituted in 1979 as a measure to curb population growth and improve living standards, but it has resulted in a gender imbalance with parents favoring boys for their only child. Sex selection before birth and subsequent abortions are illegal but widely practiced, as is a policy of less-aggressive medical intervention when female children are ill. As a result, there are now 37 million more males than females in China, and in the under-eighteen age group, there are 18 million more boys than girls.[3] The effect of this sex imbalance has had a potentially disastrous effect on Chinese society, with socially disruptive behavior and increasing mental health problems among men unable to find wives. Tragically, this scarcity of women has put them at far greater risk from male violence, with increased rates of trafficking and kidnapping of women for marriage and a rise in the number of commercial sex workers in China.[4]

## I Don't—but No One's Listening

*Marriage shall only be entered into with the free and full consent of the intending spouses.*

Universal Declaration of Human Rights,
Article 16 (2)

### Jasvinder Sanghera's Story

Jasvinder comes from a Sikh family in the North of England. Her father arrived from the Punjab in the 1950s and all his children—six daughters and one son—were born in the United Kingdom. When each of Jasvinder's older sisters reached their midteens, a suitable match was found for them; a photograph would arrive in the post, beautiful material was bought, and then the girl would slip quietly away to India one day. When the turn came for the next sister above Jasvinder, it really hit home: "We didn't dare ask questions about why this was happening . . . She was taken out of school, sent abroad to get married and then she went back to school and was put in my year. No one asked any questions."

When Jasvinder was fourteen, she was shown the photograph of her intended husband, but she rebelled and later ran away from home. Her family disowned her, and she now runs Karma Nirvana, which provides help and a place of refuge for Asian women who are forced into marriages they do not want or who are escaping from violent husbands. She was too late to help her older sister Robina, who one night poured kerosene over herself and set it alight. She died from the horrific injuries.[5]

*What does an adolescent learn on the day of their forced wedding? That their body and their life no longer belong to them.*

—Marie-Hélène Franjou, French pediatrician[6]

In a forced marriage, one or both parties do not give full, informed, and free consent to the marriage. In some cultures, girls as young as seven are engaged to much older boys or men whom they might not even meet until they marry many years later. Forced marriage often condones a culture of physical and mental violence, rape, and cruelty from the parents-in-law, with consequent misery and psychological harm to the woman involved. This all goes on behind closed doors, at home, in the marriage bed, and observed by relations—so there is no place of safety or refuge, and a marriage can become a prison. The misery of an impending forced marriage or the subsequent reality can lead to eating problems, deteriorating mental health, self-harm, attempted suicide, and loss of identity. Most cases involve young women and girls between the ages of thirteen and thirty although there is evidence to suggest that as many as 15 percent of victims are male.[7]

## Rape within Marriage

Marital rape was only made a criminal act in the United Kingdom in 1991. Until then it was considered impossible for a man to rape or sexually assault his wife; the prevailing opinion was that he was merely, and justifiably, demanding his conjugal rights:

> A husband cannot rape his wife unless the parties are separated or the court has by injunction forbidden him to interfere with his wife or he has given an undertaking in court not to interfere with her.[8]

In 1993, the UN Declaration on the Elimination of Violence against Women established marital rape as a human rights violation, but not all member states have signed the declaration and instituted criminal penalties. In Malaysia, for instance, Section 375 of the Penal Code provides without exception—even if she is unwilling or forced—that sexual intercourse by a man with a woman to whom he is married is not rape.[9]

## Breaking the Silence: Domestic Violence

*Judge: Sir, you have used violence against a person.*
*Man: That's not a person, that's my wife.*[10]

Domestic violence is only one aspect of violence against women, but it is perhaps the most hidden and secretive abuse men use against their wives, partners, sisters, and daughters in the place women and girls should feel safest—the home. It has remained hidden for so long for many reasons, including the stigma involved in asking for help and the historical indifference of both society and its legal frameworks designed to address the problem. In the past it has been treated as a private issue, and a problem that the state shouldn't get involved with.

## I Hardly Touched Her . . .

> *I . . . tried to provide evidence of his violence but it was particularly difficult because he was careful to hit me in places where it left fewer traces (punches in the stomach) and the few medical certificates I was able to use did not say much.*

> —Mrs. N, testimony obtained
> by Amnesty International[11]

Definitions of domestic violence vary—and ideas about what constitutes it also vary according to where you are in the world. The British Home Office revised its own definition in 2004 to include violence between family members over eighteen, as well as adults who are, or were, intimate partners. This means it can now encompass issues such as honor-based violence and forced marriage. It also follows the same definition that the British police use:

> " Any incident of threatening behavior, violence or abuse (psychological, physical, sexual, financial or emotional) between adults who are or have been intimate partners or family members, regardless of gender or sexuality.

Domestic abuse includes actual or threatened physical violence, sexual assault, stalking, intimidation, keeping a partner from contacting family or friends, stopping them from working outside the home, and continuous use of abusive and derogatory language. Domestic violence can be physical, sexual, or psychological abuse—but it always involves humiliation, denigration, and pain. Violence in the home against women is a denial of their basic human rights to security, equality, liberty, and sometimes even the right to life itself.

In the United States, between 2,800 and 3,000 women are murdered by men each year—that is roughly the same as the number of people who were killed in the terrorist attacks of September 11, 2001. Yet this annual death toll has provoked no war on domestic violence in America.[12] The easy availability of guns and the gun culture exacerbate the problem; a woman is two and a half times more likely to be shot by her male partner than she is to be killed by any other means in the United States.

In Jamaica, rape is a criminal offense punishable with a prison sentence, unless it occurs within marriage; then a woman has no protection at all. In the first ten months of 2005, 16 percent of reported rapes in Jamaica were at gunpoint.[13]

## Living in Fear

Women who experience domestic violence may be frightened that they'll lose their homes and children if they complain to the authorities. In Britain, if women who are foreign nationals and in the country legally do not themselves have citizenship, immigration laws provide them no recourse to public funds. Shelters are publicly funded, so these women can't even go to a shelter. They fear that by speaking out they will forfeit their right to remain in the country and will have to return to their country of origin with the shame of having failed in their chance for a better life for themselves and their children. In some cases, a woman might be accused of having dishonored her family and would be perceived as having become an unattractive, undesirable, and unmarriageable financial burden.[14]

## Turning a Blind Eye

Russia has a very high incidence of domestic violence, which has been attributed to residual influence of the *Domostroi*—a manual on how to discipline a wife, family, and servants written in the sixteenth century. During the tsarist era, wife beating was condoned, but following the revolution of 1917, the Bolsheviks at least paid lip service to improving the situation. Since 1989 and the fall of the Soviet Union, domestic violence has seen a renaissance again, triggered largely by economic hardship and political instability.[15] In 2003 the Russian government reported that 9,000 women had died at the hands of a current or former partner, a rate of one death every hour.[16]

In 2003 the Russian parliament, or Duma, wrote to Amnesty International and stated that it, along with a large percentage of the population, would consider a law against violence in the family an infringement on private

---

### Liuba's Story

---

One night her husband came home drunk and was so angry at being served only potatoes for dinner that he threw the vegetables into the corridor, shouting, "I earn enough money to deserve better food!" He then beat her, and when the children tried to intervene he beat them as well. "Our small daughter was between me and him and I thought he would kill her. We tried to barricade one of the rooms but he broke the door open. The children were screaming. Somehow we got out of the flat and went to my father-in-law. The next morning my father-in-law went to see Oleg and when he came back he simply said, 'You did not serve your husband well; I don't want to get involved in your marital problems.' My husband thinks I am his possession, that he owns me and that I have to endure everything because I am his wife."[17]

---

family matters, and therefore would not pursue the implementation of such a law. However, since 1998, the Moscow Women's Crisis Center has existed as a last resort for abused women in the city.

### Slipping through the Net: Julia, Alan, and William Pemberton

*"Oh God, I have about one minute before I die. Oh my God, help me."*

—the last words of Julia Pemberton

In some cases it has proved alarmingly easy for the police and other social services to fail abused women who are victims of domestic violence, even in countries where recourse to law and preventative measures are easily available.

In November 2003, Julia Pemberton rang the UK emergency telephone number, 999, fearing an attack by her estranged husband, Alan—who was already banned by a court order from being anywhere near the house. The police told her to "stay hidden" and said they were on the way. However, they delayed six hours before entering the house that night, by which time Alan Pemberton had already shot his wife and his sixteen-year-old son, William, before turning the gun on himself. Julia's brother, Frank Mullane, blames the police for failing his sister—"the very organization Julia trusted to save her life was instrumental in ensuring she lost it." Fourteen months earlier, Julia had gone to the police when Alan had threatened to kill her after years of abuse. As so often in similar cases, the warning signs were there all along, but no coherent plan to protect her was put in place. Frank Mullane campaigns to change the way authorities act in cases of domestic violence: "It's not just about my sister and nephew—it is about how we stop the next woman from dying next week."[18]

## Breaking Taboos: Bringing Help

The way forward in combating domestic violence is to provide a framework of legal rights to protect women in their own homes and to educate both men and women about what they can do to stop abuse. The police, public prosecutors, social workers, and doctors all need to be educated in order to recognize what is considered acceptable conflict within an intimate relationship. Most of all, women and their children need a place of safety to escape to and the support to break free and speak out. Male attitudes about ownership and abuse of their female relatives need to be challenged, countered, and, in the event of domestic violence, prosecuted by law.

It's also important to recognize the small, but nonetheless important, numbers of men abused by their female partners, and children who abuse their elderly parents—vulnerable minorities who also need help and may be hampered from seeking it due to shame and fear of ridicule or stigma.

## Escape

Angela Penney was abused for twenty-five years: "When you're in this kind of relationship, you know it's wrong, but you can't see any way out."[19]

It's important to have emergency medical centers where victims of domestic violence can go; women may prefer going to a more anonymous center, as they might feel embarrassed going their local doctors who know them and their families well. Special women's police stations have been set up in several countries in an attempt to make them more accessible to women—the first was in São

Paulo, Brazil, in 1985. Its success encouraged other South American countries to do the same, and now versions of these exist in Malaysia, Spain, Pakistan, and India.

There are also growing initiatives for centers that offer women immediate access to all the various services they may need—police, doctors, counselors, lawyers, probation officers, social workers, housing providers, education support workers, and children's services—all in one place and under one roof, and often with on-site day care centers and cafés. The first was the San Diego Family Justice Center set up in 2005 in California, and a similar one was established that same year in Croydon, near London. These centers offer solutions to breaking the cycle of domestic abuse rather than the short-term protection offered in women's shelters.

## Honor Killings

Murders in the name of "honor" are murders where, predominantly, women are killed, usually by family members or killers contracted by the family, for perceived sins of immodesty or immoral behavior. The women involved are considered to have breached a family code of honor and brought shame on its members. An honor killing may be the culmination of years of abuse and violence or the result of a single act, but such killings occur throughout the world, in Europe, the Middle East, Latin America, and South Asia, and across different religious communities from Christianity to Sikhism and Islam. There is growing international recognition that these honor killings need to be placed within the broader framework of violence against women, in the same way as female genital mutilation has been, rather than just being viewed as being a particular crime of a specific culture or community.[20]

> " The Government of Pakistan vigorously condemns the practise of so-called "honour-killing." Such actions do not find any place in our religion or law.
>
> —General Pervez Musharraf, President of Pakistan (2001–2001) at the National Convention on Human Rights and Human Dignity, 2000

Despite President Musharraf's assurance, recent studies say that honor killings, or Karo-Kari as they're called in Pakistan, are still carried out there. Madadgaar Helpline (an Urdu word meaning "helper") is Pakistan's first UNICEF-sponsored helpline for abused women and children. In 2006 it reported a total of 1,305 honor killings—792 were women, 472 were men, 34 were underage girls, and 7 were underage boys. Of the total, 1,064 cases were registered at various police stations, but many of the culprits had not been arrested, showing a lack of interest on the part of the police to provide protection and to conduct a proper investigation.[21]

In 2004, Turkey—under pressure from women's groups, the European Union, and the media—launched a government campaign to outlaw honor killings. The

Turkish penal code has been strengthened to make it illegal to even plan an honor killing, let alone carry one out. Nevertheless, despite the government's best efforts, a Turkish parliamentary report in August 2006 found that 1,091 honor killings had been committed in the past five years—more than four each week. Another study interviewed fifty-one honor killers, only three of whom expressed any regret for what they had done. Women activists blame the patriarchal and feudal system that exists in rural Turkey and the problems of refugee families living on top of each other in camps, where instances of rape and incest have escalated. In the southeast area of the country, near Diyarbakir, where many of the honor killings take place, vulnerable women are offered protection through emergency telephone hotlines and shelters. The first government-run shelter opened two years ago, and many of the women who go there are pregnant teenage rape victims, who risk being killed by relatives who blame them (but not their rapists) for what has happened.[22]

## Sex outside Marriage

*You shall not commit adultery.*

—Exodus 20:14

*. . . with all the townspeople assembled and leveling their stern regards at Hester Prynne,—yes, at herself—who stood on the scaffold of the pillory, an infant on her arm,*

*and the letter A, in scarlet, fantastically embroidered with*
*gold thread, upon her bosom!*

—Nathaniel Hawthorne's shamed heroine
in *The Scarlet Letter*[23]

Throughout history, the adulteress has always been an object of fascination and revulsion by the rest of society. For Nathaniel Hawthorne's fictional character Hester Prynne, the punishment for her adultery meant wearing a scarlet letter A sewn to her dress in her strait-laced, sin-obsessed Puritan New England community. Other societies have meted out less literal, but equally cruel and ostracizing, penalties for unsanctioned sex. From Biblical stories, Norse myths, and ancient Greek mythology—right through to the current fascination and prurient interest in celebrity culture—the woman who strays from the marital bed is almost always the target of vilification. Her husband, the cuckold, is viewed with a mixture of pity and derision, and the man with whom she has extramarital sex generally escapes all blame—at worst he's seen as an opportunist, at best an irresistible Casanova figure.

If it's the man who commits adultery, the woman he sleeps with is usually portrayed as a temptress, a "marriage breaker," dangerous and highly immoral. His wife may be pitied, but there's often something more subtle going on as well—hints that it was her fault her husband had an affair; such hints suggest that that she had allowed herself to get fat, become less sexually attractive, had put the children first, had become narrow-minded and obsessed with housework, had in fact bored her partner into someone else's bed, so that his adultery is somehow condoned and understood. Men and women are rarely viewed equally around the world when it comes to adultery.

> **Want to save your marriage? Ignore your children!**

This was a headline in a national British newspaper, which went on to describe how the female author had been propositioned by three would-be male adulterers in one week, and they all gave her the same reason for straying from the marriage bed: "She never has any time for me these days. Our sex life has more or less evaporated. What with her work and the kids, it's like she doesn't even know I'm there."[24]

### Zina

*Zina* is the word for extramarital sex, "crimes against chastity," or "immoral relations" outside of marriage under some interpretations of Islamic law around the world.

In Pakistan, a set of draconian laws called the Hudood Ordinance was brought into the country's penal code in 1979 under the then leader, General Muhammad Zia ul-Haq. They were laws intended to make the criminal justice system conform with Islamic law and covered offenses including zina laws. The Hudood laws were most criticized for the way they equated rape with adultery and made rape very difficult to prove. The law required a full confession from the man, or four male witnesses of good character who were prepared to testify. This meant that in practice very few women brought a man to court for rape, and very few men confessed and were successfully prosecuted. The following story is a combination of several different cases from Pakistan.

Priya, age thirteen, was abducted and raped by her neighbor. Her brother found her bruised and unconscious in an alley behind their house. Her father reported the rape at the police station, and medical reports confirmed that she had been sexually assaulted. The case was brought before a magistrate.

Priya named her attacker but had no proof of rape other than the medical examination . . . Priya's neighbor denied the charges of rape and so she was unable to prove that the act of penetration had been nonconsensual.

Because she had started menstruating a few months earlier, Priya was legally considered an adult; a medical examination proved that penetration did occur and she was put in detention on charges of zina herself; her father also faced charges for reporting the rape while Priya's rapist went free.[25]

In November 2006, the Women's Protection Bill was passed by the Pakistan parliament, intending to amend the Hudood Ordinance on rape. Progressive groups in the country welcomed the bill, but they are concerned that it doesn't go far enough. The new laws say that all accusations concerning rape and adultery will be heard by a judge in court who will then decide whether there is

### Iran: The Case of Atefeh Rejabi Sahaaleh[26]

On August 15, 2004, a sixteen-year-old Iranian girl was hanged from a crane in a public square in her hometown of Neka in northern Iran, executed after receiving the death sentence for "crimes against chastity." A BBC documentary claimed that Atefeh Rejabi Sahaaleh's age was put at twenty-two in the Supreme Court papers relating to her case.[27] Iran has signed an international treaty that prohibits the death sentence for those under the age of eighteen. She said she had been raped repeatedly by a fifty-one-year old taxi-driver, Ali Darabi, a married man with children. He got ninety-five lashes. Rape is very hard to prove in an Iranian court:

> Men's word is accepted much more clearly and much more easily than women . . . They can say, "You know she encouraged me, or she didn't wear proper dress."
> —Iranian lawyer and exile
> Mohammad Hoshi[28]

There are fears that public hangings are increasing under President Mahmoud Ahmadinejad. Shirin Ebadi, the Iranian human rights lawyer and 2003 winner of the Nobel Peace Prize says that recently there have been at least fourteen other cases of public hangings of women for crimes against chastity. She is concerned that the threat of public hangings is being used as a weapon of fear by the state against activists and opposition groups.

enough evidence to pursue an investigation. While women will feel safer reporting a rape in sessions court rather than at a police station, in rural areas they will have to travel much farther to reach a court, which may well deter them. Imrana Khwaja, lawyer and former human rights activist says, "It's going to change things, but not a great deal."[29]

## After the Affair

Adultery often leads to the breakdown of a marriage and culminates in divorce if permitted by the religion of both partners. In the West there are websites, magazines, lawyers by the thousand, and self-help groups all devoted to helping people cope with divorce. Even in countries where divorce is relatively acceptable, religious beliefs, cultural strictures, and financial considerations often stop men and women from getting out of unhappy marriages.

Added to this is the reality that women suffer disproportionately after divorce or relationship breakdown, and that they are usually the ones who bring up the children. In Australia, for example, over 14 percent of households are single-parent families; they form the lowest economic segment of society, and their children are the most disadvantaged with the worst life prospects. This pattern is repeated all over the world. Just as adultery in general is harder on women, so too is divorce. The divorced woman, often caring for her children alone, is seen as a burden on society. A man who chooses to live with or marry a woman who has children from a former marriage is viewed by society as a mixture of hero and gullible fool—the insinuation is that he has been trapped or snared for his money, especially if the man is younger than the woman. If a woman marries a divorced man who has children in tow, it's understood that she is there to mother the children: that is her role in return for the economic security of marriage. If she doesn't fulfill her role, she is cast as the "evil stepmother," a character common throughout societies and fiction in any age and any part of the world.

Although, in general, divorce is more common and more accepted in the West, there is often stigma, public shame, and disproportionate economic hardship for divorced women all over the world—and for some there is the additional obstacle of the women's family having to repay her bride price. Added to all this, discriminatory laws in some countries also make it difficult or nearly impossible for women to prove grounds for divorce:

> " The women of Uganda can now cheat. That seems to have been the signal that the Uganda High Court sent to married women last week.
> —*The Nation* newspaper in Kenya,
> April 14, 2007

The Ugandan Constitutional Court made a breakthrough ruling in March 2007, declaring that its current divorce law was discriminatory and therefore inconsistent with the constitution. Activists had been campaigning for change for the last four years—saying that the previously existing law was unfair to women. Under the old law, a married man could legally have an affair with an unmarried woman, but if a married woman did the same with an unmarried man she had committed a crime. This was punishable by a fine or up to a year in prison and gave her husband enough grounds for divorce. Previously, adultery on its own had not been sufficient grounds for a woman to divorce her husband in Uganda; in addition she had to prove that she had been mistreated or deserted.

## Religion and Divorce

In the Roman Catholic Church, there are strict guidelines about divorce. The church sees the bond of marriage as sacred, as both a legal bond on earth and as a spiritual bond, which God has sanctified. So a Catholic cannot receive Holy Communion if he or she remarries. This is particularly difficult for devout Catholics who feel that the Eucharist is central to their faith, and in some predominately Catholic countries, to be a divorcee is still a matter of public shame. Saint Augustine made the Catholic position clear in the fifth century, and not much has changed since: "The compact of marriage is not done away by divorce intervening; so that they continue wedded persons one to another, even after separation; and commit adultery with those, with whom they shall be joined, even after their own divorce."[30]

From its inception, Islam accepted that there could be divorce, and the Koran advises men who divorce their wives to leave them with respect. Although culturally in some Islamic countries divorced women are considered to have failed, in terms of their faith they have not committed any sin by divorcing or being divorced.

## Married for Life

Similar to Catholic attitudes to divorce, in the Hindu and Sikh religions, men and women are married for life; a marriage is a union of two families, two sets of ancestors, and a sacred bond. So divorce is a rupture of not just a personal relationship, but also of familial and economic alliances, expectations, and ideas of ownership. The resulting separation and breaking of the marriage bond may well affect women disproportionately for many of the reasons this chapter has tried to explore.

## Female Genital Mutilation

*I was taken to a very dark room and undressed. I was blindfolded and stripped naked . . . I was forced to lie flat on my back by four strong women, two holding tight to each leg. Another woman sat on my chest to prevent my upper body from moving. A piece of cloth was forced in my mouth to stop me screaming. I was then shaved. When [it] began, I put up a big fight. The pain was terrible and unbearable. During this fight I was badly cut and lost blood. All those who took part . . . were half drunk with alcohol.*[31]

Hannah Koroma from Sierra Leone was ten when her genitals were cut in the way she describes. She is just one of the 2 million young girls who undergo female genital mutilation, or FGM, each year, joining the 130 million women worldwide who have already been cut.[32] FGM is a deep-rooted cultural tradition in parts of Africa, the Middle East, and Asia.

> " FGM is an issue that concerns women and men who believe in equality, dignity and fairness to all human beings, regardless of gender, race, religion or ethnic identity. It must not be seen as the problem of any one group or culture, whether African, Muslim or Christian. FGM is practiced by many cultures. It represents a human tragedy and must not be used to set Africans against non-Africans, one religious group against the other, or even women against men.
> —Nahid Toubia, *A Call for Global Action*[33]

FGM is an extreme form of violence against women, a way of controlling their sexuality cloaked as a traditional, and therefore accepted and sanctioned, behavior.

> " [Excision] shows an attempt to confer an inferior status on women by branding them with this mark which diminishes them and is a constant reminder to them that they are only women, inferior to men, that they do not even have any rights over their own bodies or fulfillment either

> bodily or personal. As we can view male circumcision as being a measure of hygiene, in same way we can only see excision as a measure of inferiorization.
> —Thomas Sankara, former president of Burkina Faso from 1983 until his assassination in 1987. His government banned female genital mutilation and promoted contraception—his was also the first African state to publicly recognize the threat of HIV/AIDS.

Despite the fact that FGM is legally banned across much of Africa, it is still common practice in about thirty countries there. The rituals vary from country to country in terms of the age at which girls are cut and what it signifies in the community, whether coming of age, sexual maturity, or cleanliness. The World Health Organization suggests that girls are undergoing FGM at a younger and younger age, and that whereas girls used to be cut when they were about seventeen or eighteen, the age has been dropping to between six and ten.[34]

## What FGM Involves

There are different degrees of FGM—all generally carried out without any recognized anesthetic. The most extreme form involves the excision of the clitoris and the labia minora, and the stitching of the vaginal opening (infibulation) so it becomes a tiny hole, only big enough to allow urine and menstrual blood to pass through. Infibulation means women often have constant problems with urinary tract and other infections for the rest of their lives; it can take them a long time to urinate. For childbirth, which is more risky for women who have undergone FGM, they have to be cut open again and resewn afterwards. Girls who have been cut have an increased risk of contracting HIV/AIDS, because it is more likely that their genitals will tear during intercourse, which means the virus can pass far more easily between partners. Sexual intercourse is often extremely painful for the women. In the most tragic cases, FGM can result in massive hemorrhaging, blood loss, and shock sufficient to kill the girl. The custom of cutting several girls at one time exacerbates the risk of disease transmission, as the same knife is used for each without being cleaned. If FGM is carried out in remote rural areas, there is scant chance of getting any medical help should something go wrong.

## Cultural Pressures

With FGM, there is a thin dividing line between consent and having no realistic choice. A mother may not want her daughter to suffer as she has, but she sees little alternative if her daughter is not to be ostracized by the community. In order to be accepted and find a marriage partner in these communities, a girl must undergo FGM. It confers significance on the girls, giving them cultural pride and status. In some communities the clitoris is regarded as unclean and a symbol of masculinity.

For a long time FGM, like domestic violence, was a hidden aspect of women's lives. Outside intervention to try to question or prevent it was seen as a form of cultural imperialism, an unwelcome intrusion into a traditional way of life. FGM cuts right across class and economic conditions—wealthy and middle-class Asian, Middle Eastern, and African girls are cut, as well as girls living in extreme poverty in the villages.

The 1993 UN World Conference on Human Rights in Vienna placed FGM firmly in the center of a human rights debate rather than viewing it as a private issue:

> It is unacceptable that the international community remain passive in the name of a distorted vision of multiculturalism. Human behaviours and cultural values, however senseless or destructive they may appear from the personal and cultural standpoint of others, have meaning and fulfill a function for those who practise them. However, culture is not static but it is in constant flux, adapting and reforming. People will change their behaviour when they understand the hazards and indignity of harmful practices and when they realize that it is possible to give up harmful practices without giving up meaningful aspects of their culture.[35]

In recent years, FGM has been recognized by the international community as a fundamental breach of a woman's human rights, a form of violent torture, however deeply rooted it is in a country's traditions. But the fact that it's a taboo subject, not usually discussed between the sexes, can lead to a communication gap. Some men may have been educated about the dangers of the practice and are happy for it to be abandoned, but they avoid discussing this taboo subject with their wives. Therefore, women carry on believing that it's necessary for their daughters to be cut, just as they were in their turn.

### Change from Within

Legislation and international communiqués outlawing FGM can only work in cooperation with a willingness among communities to change; otherwise, nothing will eradicate the process. In 1997 in Senegal, in a small village called Malicounda Bambara, the women began to start talking openly about FGM and the health issues it entails under the guidance of an NGO called Tostan (which means breakthrough). All the community joined in, including the men, the village elders, and the "cutters," and after much discussion FGM was denounced. Two years later it was abolished and the cutters were found other jobs to enable them to make a living. The courage of this community had a ripple effect and now one hundred other communities in Senegal have also banned FGM.

During one of these ceremonies, held on the island of Niodior, men, women, and children from all the twenty-six islands of the Sine-Saloum River in Senegal met to agree on a declaration to abandon cutting. Rockaya Diene, representing all the women's groups of the participating islands, took the microphone:

> At a certain point, we women realized that this practice could no longer continue. We met together and spoke of this as a problem that is sapping our society and poisoning our life. We admitted the health problems we have encountered, we women who have already been cut. And we found a solution together—to forever end this butcher-like practice.

Then the traditional cutters wrapped their knives in cloth to hide them because they are considered sacred, and threw them into a straw basket, symbolizing the end of FGM in their community.[36]

## FGM in the Hospital

"The war against FGM appears to be going round in circles, as physicians take it up." This is what Julie Maranya, director of a Nairobi-based women's rights organization said about the relatively recent but growing phenomenon of FGM being performed by doctors under proper medical supervision.

Some young girls are being brought to hospitals where they undergo FGM in a medically safe environment carried out by trained doctors, at a higher cost than the traditional village cutters. The health advantages are obvious, and its proponents argue that if FGM is going to be carried out anyway, then it's far better for it to take place in these relatively safe and hygienic conditions. This trend is exacerbated by the shift toward urban living and by parents becoming more concerned about the health issues involved and more careful about how their daughters are cut. Today, 94 percent of parents in Egypt who want their daughters cut arrange for them to undergo this "medicalized" form of FGM, in addition to 76 percent of parents in Yemen, 65 percent in Mauritania, 48 percent in Côte d'Ivoire, and 46 percent in Kenya.[37] However, women's rights activists counter this by saying the pro-medicalization argument is retroactive and undoes all the hard work they do in trying to change attitudes and practices within communities at a grassroots level.

## Designer Vaginas

While young girls undergo the intense pain of FGM every day, some women, mainly in the West, elect to have vaginal surgery—not infibulation, but labial tucks and reductions performed by a plastic surgeon, called labiaplasty. Dr. Pamela Loftus has been performing these operations for over twenty years in Florida, and reports that recently she's been avalanched with requests from young women wanting vaginal cosmetic surgery, perhaps not at their own volition:

> " The most common reason we hear is that they have had a negative comment made by a male sexual partner. Women are made to feel that

> they are not perfect the way they are and often
> it's the partner that sets this off.[38]

It used to be mainly sex workers or swimwear models who opted for labial surgery, under pressure from images of supposedly perfect labia in porn magazines and films. Now increasing numbers of women from all professions and at any age are trying it out. They associate sagging or loose labia with old age, with childbirth, and with being sexually undesirable. There is another cosmetic procedure, which involves tightening the vagina and perineum area, which some doctors claim gives increased sexual pleasure for both partners. However, there is a risk of cutting the nerves involved and of enduring a great amount of pain and ending up with bad scarring, as with any surgical procedure.

Whether performed for cultural or cosmetic purposes, without a woman's agreement or by her own free choice, genital alteration generally seems to be in the context of men passing judgment over how a women's genitals should look and function, disregarding the terrible pain and life-long difficulties that cutting her will bring.

## Widows and Witches

*Three women, all members of the same family, were killed after an angry mob of villagers accused them of practicing witchcraft at Lusikisiki, Eastern Cape police said on Friday.*

> *The seventy-year-old woman, her daughter aged fifty-six
> and a twenty-six-year-old granddaughter were stabbed to
> death with bush knives and other objects on Wednesday
> night, spokesman Captain Zamukulungisa Jozana said.
> The mob of villagers who believed they were witches held
> them captive at the Gura locality from 4PM to 8PM and
> then killed them. No arrests have been made and police
> are investigating three cases of murder.*

—South African Press Association, April 20, 2007

## Women and Witchcraft

Historically, witches in Europe were portrayed as female, either widowed or single, often sexually voracious and disrupters of society and of families. Women, with their supposed inferior intellect and inherent moral weakness, were seen as more susceptible than men to the temptations of the Devil, and readier to make a pact with him to gain supernatural powers over the lives of others. The "Malleus Maleficarum," or "Hammer of Witches," published in the 1480s, was a viciously misogynist handbook on how to identify, prosecute, and punish female witches. This famous document from the late Middle Ages influenced the next two centuries of frenzied witch hunts in Europe.

By conducting witch hunts and trials, and creating outcasts, societies have always made scapegoats out of vulnerable individuals in order to appease mass hysteria. From the 1692 witch trials in Salem, Massachusetts that inspired Arthur Miller's play *The Crucible,* to the frenzied

*Illustration of a seventeenth century witch trial. © 2009 Jupiterimages Corporation.*

anticommunist purges of 1950s America, and including the witch hunting that still exists today in some parts of the world, certain women have been singled out and vilified by whole communities.

## The Witches of Gambaga

In Northern Ghana today, more than 1,000 women live in exile in six camps. One of these, Gambaga, has existed since 1700. These women are outcasts, accused of witchcraft by their villages. The male chief at Gambaga has a ritual for the arrival of each new woman: a guinea fowl is slaughtered in her honor. If it falls forward as it dies, the woman is a witch, if backwards, she's innocent and can return to her community, although in practice she rarely does. The women who make it to the villages are the lucky ones; the unlucky ones are stoned or lynched at home before they can escape. These women are usually post-menopausal and seen as useless by their communities. They may be accused of causing illness or harm to a family member. After a recent bout of cerebrospinal meningitis in Ghana, which was subsequently blamed on witchcraft, there was an influx of women sent to the villages.[39] Some of them bring a granddaughter to the camp to help them; this girl will not attend school, and it is often dangerous for her to return to her village after her grandmother's death as she may be branded a witch by association. Stopping this practice is about educating communities, about combating superstitious beliefs that malign forces are at work in women, but it's also about addressing the wider issue of gender discrimination and violence.

> People are becoming better aware that these issues are not just metaphysical but also a human rights issue.
> —Richard Quayson, deputy commissioner of the Commission on Human Rights and Administrative Justice (CHRAJ), Ghana's leading human rights organization

## Widows

The status of women without men is frequently ambiguous. Widows, unlike widowers, generally have a very low social status. They are often financially dependent on male relatives and are at risk of losing their homes and property after their husbands die.

India has over 40 million widows. Although the 1856 Hindu Widows Remarriage Act gave women the legal right to remarry and the Hindu Succession Act of 1956 gave women the same inheritance rights as men, those rights are rarely put into practice. Once widowed, a woman's lack of social or economic status often reduces her to destitution. Deepak Mehta's film *Water* (2006) highlights the plight of widows who are sent to ashrams, or the holy cities in the north—Vrindavan and Varanasi—and have to exist by begging for the rest of their lives. Some of these women were child brides, promised to husbands who then died, and they are condemned to this life before they have experienced any other.

### Jumping onto the Flames

*Sati,* the traditional Hindu practice of a woman throwing herself on her husband's funeral pyre, is thought to have originated 700 years ago among the warrior class—the Rajputs—when the men died in battle and their wives immolated themselves in order to avoid being taken captive by the victors. Later, sati was seen as a virtuous and unselfish act that absolved a woman's ancestors from all their past sins. Women who committed sati were worshipped in India. The practice was first banned in 1829, but it had to be rebanned in 1956 after a resurgence, and yet another prevention ordinance was passed in 1987. It is now illegal to even be a bystander at a sati ceremony, and it is extremely rare. The most controversial case, which caused national and international outrage, occurred in Rajasthan in 1987 when an eighteen-year-old girl, Roop Kanwar, burned to death.[40] The girl's father-in-law and brother-in-law were charged with forcing her to sit on the pyre, but nine years later they were acquitted. The last recorded case was in August 2006, when a forty-year-old woman, Janakrani, burned to death on the funeral pyre of her husband, Prem Narayan, in the Sagar district of Madhya Pradesh.

Self-immolation continues, but it has become a hidden shame. A wife may burn herself if she's in an unhappy marriage, as a way out of extreme domestic violence, or

because of persistent cruelty from her husband's family—
she may even be burned by someone else within the home.
These deaths are often explained away as accidents in the
kitchen or home; for instance, kerosene lamps falling over
and burning women to death. There are thousands of
these "accidents" reported each year; one women's group in
the southern city of Bangalore estimates that up to five
women a day are taken to the city hospital suffering from
massive burns.[41]

### Widow Cleansing

Widows in Malawi, Nigeria, Zambia, and other African
countries, may be subjected to "widow cleansing," which
involves the widow having sex with a relative of her late
husband or the village cleanser before being allowed to remain in her home—a home that she may well have contributed to buying and has been maintaining ever since.[42]
It's a mechanism to keep property in the husband's extended family. Widow cleansing has become extremely
risky with HIV/AIDS, so families—worried about infect-
ing their own men—are now more inclined to employ a
widow cleanser, who may be carrying the disease himself
and thus infect the widow. Widows who refuse to be
cleansed can be thrown out of the home and face other
forms of discrimination. Cleansing is thought to remove
any curses put on the family, so an uncleansed widow may
not be allowed to enter people's homes for fear of bringing
evil spirits, may not be allowed to eat with other villagers,
draw water from the same source as other women, or even

walk through other people's farms for fear their crops will wilt. The NGO Human Rights Watch has called the problems of widows and property rights in sub-Saharan Africa "catastrophic." Widows who refuse to be cleansed can end up homeless, living on the streets or in slums, forced to beg for food, unable to afford healthcare or school fees for their children, and vulnerable to sexual abuse and exploitation.[43]

## Women in Prison

### Keeping Clean

*You should be able to have a hot bath or shower at least once a week. You may also be given toiletries, including feminine hygiene products, depending on the prison you are in.*

HM Prison Prisoner's Information Book:
Women and Young Offenders, 2003[44]

When women—who are often wives and mothers—are imprisoned, their families generally suffer far worse than if men are put behind bars. As women are often the main care givers in the home—looking after children as well as elderly relatives, doing the majority of the housework, cooking, nurturing—their absence has a disastrous effect on those around them.

### Women behind Bars: Some Statistics

In prisons in the United Kingdom, as in other prison systems across the world, women suffer disproportionately more than men. There are seventeen women's prisons in Britain; seven of these have mother and baby units where children can stay with their mothers until they reach either nine or eighteen months, but spaces are very limited. The female prison population in Britain is about 5.6 percent of the total, but it has more than doubled in the last ten years to around 4,200. The small number of prisons means that women are often separated from their families by longer distances than are imprisoned men, which puts additional strain on all concerned. Fifty-five percent of women in British prisons have a child under sixteen. Perhaps understandably, the mental health of incarcerated women is far worse than that of incarcerated men—up to 80 percent of women in prison have diagnosable psychiatric problems, compared to less than 20 percent in the general community.

> Women's prisons have become our social dustbins. They are now seen as a stopgap, cut-price provider of drug detox, mental health assessment and treatment—a refuge for those failed by public services . . . We are locking up our most damaged and vulnerable women in bleak, under-staffed institutions, from which, despite the best efforts of many people, they are almost bound to emerge more damaged, more vulnerable. Imprisonment will cause a third of women prisoners to lose their homes, reduce future chances of employment and shatter family ties.
> —Juliet Lyon, director of the United Kingdom Prison Reform Trust

Fifty percent of the women say they have been abused physically, emotionally, or sexually and 30 percent of all women in prison self-harm, compared to 6 percent of male prisoners. Additionally, proportionally more women than men in prisons are addicted to hard drugs.

## On the Inside

> *That was not part of my sentence, to . . . perform oral sex with the officers.*
>
> —New York prisoner Tanya Ross,
> November 1998[45]

Sexual abuse of women in prison by male guards is a violation of their human rights, but the victims often feel reluctant to complain, fearing worse retaliation from the guards if they do. There are over 148,000 women in state and federal prisons in the United States, and 70 percent of the guards who work in them are male. Allegations against the guards by female inmates include claims of rape and other types of sexual assault including sexual extortion and groping during body searches. Male guards are always watching when the women undress, have a shower, or use the toilet.[46]

## Race, Gender, Sexuality, and Prison

In the United States, an African-American woman is eight times more likely than a Caucasian woman to be imprisoned. Most are serving sentences for nonviolent drug or property-related offences. A Latina is four times more likely than a white woman to be in jail. Black women are doubly discriminated against throughout the criminal justice system because of their color and their gender. Even in daily life, they are more likely to be stopped and searched. In the United Kingdom, the Crown Prosecution Service found that the police tended to bring charges against black defendants with weaker evidence than against white people, and black defendants are also likely to be given longer sentences.[47]

The case of Robin Lucas in the United States illustrates how sexuality can affect justice and imprisonment. She was convicted of credit card fraud in California in 1995 and sent to a mainly male prison where she was visible to male prisoners and guards all day and night, even when on the toilet or in the shower. She said the guards taunted her for being a lesbian saying "maybe we can change your mind."[48] One evening, three inmates unlocked her cell door, then handcuffed and raped her. No disciplinary action was ever taken against the prisoners or against those guards who were implicated in the attack.[49] Finally Robin won a civil lawsuit for compensation in 1998. That same year the *National Law Journal* conducted a survey of jurors, asking them what factors would make them most biased against a defendant. Perceived sexual orientation came out on top, being three times more likely to influence a juror than race.

## A Groundbreaking Case

In 1989 in the United Kingdom, Kiranjit Ahluwalia set fire to her husband Deepak's bedclothes as he slept in their house, and he was burned alive.

Ten years earlier, Kiranjit's brothers had forced her to give up her law studies and agree to an arranged marriage. Deepak became violent just two days after the wedding; in the next decade his violence toward her included rape, sexual abuse; kicking; punching; beating with belts, shoes, and pieces of furniture; threats with knives and hot irons; and near strangulation. Her pleas for help were rejected by the family, who told her to be "a good wife," and "make the marriage work." She got court injunctions against Deepak, but nothing worked, and finally on May 9, 1989, Kiranjit was pushed beyond her limits and started the fire, but she said she had no intention of killing her husband.

Kiranjit lost her case because of a court gender bias toward typical male behavior in domestic conflicts. The time lapse between Deepak's last attack and Kiranjit's retaliation (a few hours) was said to be a "cooling down" period and not a "boiling over" time as her defense cited in the plea of provocation. In similar circumstances, men usually act instantaneously while women cannot because of their comparative lack of strength and physical size. Kiranjit was given a life sentence and served three years and four months before a long appeal process and retrial accepted the principle of "cumulative provocation," which was a very important legal breakthrough for other battered women. She won her case on the grounds of diminished responsibility and was released in 1992.[50]

*Photographed in June 1975, this image shows women and children in the city of Nandail, Bangladesh, during smallpox eradication efforts by the Centers for Disease Control and Prevention. Photo courtesy of the Centers for Disease Control and Prevention.*

# 3

# Health

Women's health all over the world is inextricably linked to politics, and it is usually men—whether husbands, doctors, or politicians—who make the crucial decisions that affect a woman's body. It is the most visible area of women's rights, where the personal has become a political battleground, with men historically being able to control a woman's health (and specifically her fertility) by legislating on abortion rights, contraception, and provision for maternal health-care. Unless women have the right and the power to choose how many children they have and when they have them, and unless they have confidence that they are giving birth in the safest conditions possible, they cannot assume a fully equal and active role with men in the public arena.

## Maternal Health

*Giving birth on the (Long) March was a nightmare. One woman who had gone into labour had to walk to the*

*night's destination with the baby's head dangling out.*
*Next day before dawn, weeping at leaving her baby in a*
*bundle of straw in the empty hut, she had to walk on,*
*and fainted wading through an icy river.*[1]

A woman's right to enjoy maternal healthcare is enshrined in Article 25 of the Universal Declaration of Human Rights:

> " Motherhood and childhood are entitled to special care and assistance. All children, whether born in or out of wedlock, shall enjoy the same social protection.

Women's health, particularly in childbirth, is not a given right for millions of women across the world. Apart from Sierra Leone, the most dangerous place to have a baby is Afghanistan, where for every 100,000 live births 1,900 women die—and each woman has a 1 in 6 risk of maternal death in her lifetime. This is compared to the safest country—Sweden—where there are only 2 maternal deaths per 100,000 live births, and a Swedish mother has a 1 in 29,800 chance of dying in childbirth. Each year approximately 524,000 women die worldwide from complications of pregnancy and childbirth—that's one maternal death each minute—and 99 percent of these deaths occur in conditions of poverty or in developing nations. For every woman who dies, another forty to fifty suffer serious health problems such as a fistula, a hemorrhage, a stroke, or an infection. Since the turn of the twenty-first century, there has been a decrease in infant mortality rates across the world, but this has not been matched by a decrease in maternal mortality over the same period. The World Health Organization says the underlying cause is unavailable, inaccessible, or poor quality healthcare. Maternal death has a wider impact on the children left behind. Around 1 million children are left motherless each year, and these children are ten times more likely to die in childhood than those whose mothers are still alive.

> " Pregnancy is a normal, life-affirming state. Women should not die giving birth. Their deaths are preventable, even in the poorest countries. But it takes local knowledge, strength and partnership to ensure women's lives are saved . . . One key task of the global health community is to close the gap in services for women in rich areas, and those in poor ones. If dead women are not even counted, then it seems they do not count. We have an invisible epidemic.
>
> —Dr. Joy Phumaphi, former assistant director-general of the World Health Organization

Meybeiz, a fifteen year old from Ethiopia, suffered an obstetric rupture (when the membranes between two internal cavities tear) during delivery. She was lucky—this can be a life-threatening condition and can leave the woman with permanent incontinence, but Meybeiz was brought to Addis Ababa to be treated at the only hospital in Ethiopia that treats obstetric rupture.

*A young mother and child from the Tuareg nomadic tribe. The women and children are camped in Mali awaiting the return of husbands who have gone south in search of food and water. UN photo/John Issac, 1984.*

### Meybeiz is from Ethiopia, and this is her story:

I am fifteen years old, I have had no schooling, my mother is dead; I have four sisters, two married, two are not married. I have no brother, I have no mother, I have nothing else. One day without my knowledge they married me off. There was a celebration and feasting, and my husband's family took me away. For two years I lived with my husband, and during the third year I became pregnant. I didn't know anything when I became pregnant and then I delivered. The clinic in the village said it couldn't help me because they didn't know how. The traditional birth attendant just pulled it out. The baby was not alive. I was sick, I was very sick, the urine spilled, then I came to the clinic in the city. When I recover I will go back to my father's place, not to my husband; he is not around. When I became ill, he left me and we divorced. He took me and left me at my father's. I never want to have babies again.[2]

Women and girls are susceptible to particular health risks associated with pregnancy. Early motherhood, before the girl's body is ready, can result in complicated pregnancies and risky childbirth. More than 15 million girls between the ages of fifteen and nineteen give birth each year, and the United Kingdom has the highest rate of teenage pregnancy in Europe. The lack of accurate sex education and information about and access to contraception, as well as the culture of sexual availability—where young girls may be frightened of saying no in a society that legitimizes multiple sexual partners—all exacerbate the problem, as do lack of education, poverty, and very poor prospects for employment, let alone a fulfilling career or way out of their situation.

## Contraception

*I was a young woman having my children, and I knew beyond a shadow of a doubt I didn't want a fourth child. I was given the pill, that was a major changing point in my life because for the first time in my life I could have sex and not worry about becoming pregnant . . . You can actually enjoy sex. Now some women might think that quite shocking, but why on earth are we put here if we can't enjoy sex? Men have gone out through the centuries and they have had sex and they've never been criticised for it or had to suffer for having sex outside of marriage. Before the mid-1960s, if a woman got pregnant in this country she still suffered if she had sex.*

—Maureen Dellanian, one of the
first women in Britain to use the
contraceptive pill in the 1960s.[3]

The right to control her fertility is fundamental to a woman's ability to control her own life. Finding a reliable form of contraception has been a constant preoccupation all over the world—ancient Sanskrit texts talk about extracting oil from the Neem tree, which grows prolifically across South Asia, and inserting it into the vagina to prevent pregnancy. Other manuscripts advise grinding dates and bark from the acacia tree together with honey, which is then applied to the vulva. Women were also advised to use alternatives such as olive oil, pomegranate pulp, ginger, and tobacco juice.

The diaphragm was invented in 1842 in Europe, and the first full-length rubber condom was introduced into the United States and elsewhere by the end of the 1860s, but neither of these were 100 percent reliable methods of birth control. Camel owners used to put pebbles in their female animals' uteruses, which stopped them from getting pregnant on long trips through the desert, and in 1920 this method was adapted to humans when a gynecologist named Ernst Gräfenberg developed the first proper intrauterine device, or IUD, for women, first using silk suture and then later silver wire coiled into a ring.

Advocating for birth control was an important part of early feminist campaigns for women's rights. In the United States, the nurse and writer Margaret Sanger was jailed in 1916 for opening a birth control clinic in Brooklyn, New York. In Britain, Marie Stopes published the influential *Married Love* in 1918 and advocated equality in all areas of marriage; she opened the first family planning clinic in north London three years later.

## The Pill

On August 5, 1960, the American government approved the world's first commercially produced birth control pill. This meant that for the first time, women who had access to it had a reliable method of contraception, and almost 100 percent control over their fertility. They could space the births of their children, or delay having children at all until they had established their careers or finished university degrees— something that had previously been near impossible.

Nearly ten years later, the health risks of the pill started to be acknowledged. Women had always reported side effects—some mild such as nausea and weight gain, but more serious health threats began to emerge such as blood clots, strokes, and possible links to cancer. The new generation of hormonal contraceptives prescribed today—most still in the form of a daily pill but also available via methods such as a patch, a vaginally-inserted ring, or an injection—are much safer than the first birth control pills but, as with all medication, there are still associated health risks. However, some warn that negative reaction to the pill leaves young women anxious and therefore reluctant to go on it, but still without a good, reliable alternative—therefore still at risk for unplanned pregnancies.

## Contraception and HIV/AIDS

Women and girls are particularly vulnerable to contracting HIV and AIDS for a number of reasons, partly to do with their lack of access to healthcare, social stigmatizing, gen-der-based violence, and physiology. Young women are es-pecially susceptible in South Africa, where twice as many fifteen- to twenty-four-year-old females have the virus than do males in the same age group; in Kenya and Mali women are affected at a rate four-and-a-half times that of men.[4] There is little sympathy for women who are victims of contracting a sexually transmitted disease as a result of male behavior; instead they are often perceived as being the unfaithful, promiscuous disease carriers, or simply dirty and dangerous women.

Because of the female physiology, heterosexual sex places women at greater risk than men of contracting HIV/AIDS. Semen contains higher levels of HIV than do vaginal fluids, and the composition of the vagina—with its large area of mucosal tissue—has more potential for ruptures where the virus can enter. Female genital mutilation can increase the risk of rupture and internal injuries during sex, and consequently the risk of infec-tion rises.

Research shows that women are far more likely than men to seek early diagnosis and medical intervention for HIV/AIDS—and to try to minimize the risk to others. Promiscuous men infect their wives and then blame them for seeking medical treatment that brings shame and stigma on the family. The women are doubly penalized and ostracized by the community.

There is a fallacy in parts of Africa that having sex with a virgin will "cleanse" a man who has HIV/AIDS;

subsequently, there is a reported pattern of abuse by men who target and rape minors in the hope of such a cure.[5]

## The Female Condom

As a response to these appalling health statistics in Africa over failing contraception or lack of access to it, there have been concerted efforts to give women back some control over AIDS transmission by distribution of female condoms there. This is a dual-use barrier method—it functions as a contraceptive and as a means of preventing the spread of AIDS. The female condom looks like a baggy plastic sheath with a ring at both ends; one end is inserted high up near the cervix and the other near the entrance to the vagina. One study estimated that perfect use of the female condom might reduce the annual risk of acquiring HIV by more than 90 percent among women who have intercourse twice weekly with an infected male. The female condom, marketed as Femidom, was originally launched in 1992 in the United Kingdom with a £1 million advertising campaign and the publicity headline "Johnny's had a sex change"—referring to the colloquial name for a male condom, the "rubber Johnny." Today, however, usage of the female condom is so low in the United Kingdom that it registers as 0 percent in national statistics. It is the most unpopular contraceptive because of its size and the need to insert it manually, and anecdotally, because of the particular noise, or rustle, that is said to occur during intercourse with a Femidom. However, what is being rejected in the West has been seized on as a life-saver in Africa and parts of Asia. In Zimbabwe a new word, *kaytecyenza,* has been coined to describe the tickle of the inner ring rubbing against the penis, and it is marketed as a sex toy as well as a contraceptive. Demand for the female condom is growing in countries and places where women cannot easily rely on or negotiate safe sex with their partners. The largest barriers to its more frequent use are cost and accessibility.[6]

## Abortion

*Abortionite Temple/ Human Sacrifice Practiced Here*
*"Pro-Choice": History's Most Repulsive Euphemism*
    *Since "Final Solution"*
*Life begins at conception*
*Half the patients entering an abortion clinic never come*
    *out alive*
*Abortion is to Freedom as Pornography is to Love*
*"Pro-Choice"/ Putrid Lie/ Babies NEVER/ Choose To*
    *Die!*
*Roe Vs Wade: Malice Aforethought*
            —Anti-Abortion Campaign Slogans[7]

### Roe v. Wade

In 1971 Jane Roe, a pregnant women living in Texas in the United States, went to court for the right terminate her pregnancy. At that time, Texas law prohibited abortions except in cases where the woman's life was threatened. She fought her case against Henry Wade, the district attorney of Dallas County. Two years later, the Supreme Court of the United States ruled that a woman's right to an abortion (up to three months' gestation) fell within the right to privacy protected by the 14th Amendment to the Constitution of the United States—in other words, abortion is a constitutionally protected right. In the meantime Jane Roe, whose real name is Norma McCorvey, had given birth and had her baby adopted.

*Roe v. Wade* was a landmark decision; it overturned all state and federal laws banning abortions in the United States. The case also prompted a national debate that is still going on in the twenty-first century about the role of the state in permitting abortion. The antiabortion views of the religious right and pro-life movements have led to violent demonstrations outside abortion clinics. Since 1991, three doctors and four clinic workers have been murdered. Supporters of *Roe v. Wade* assert the necessity of protecting women's equality and freedom by protecting their right to choose an abortion. However, the Supreme Court decision remains under constant attack, and many states have passed laws restricting abortions, including requirements such as forcing a young pregnant woman seeking an abortion to inform her parents or a judge, or imposing a waiting time between visiting the abortion clinic and carrying out the procedure. In March 2006, the governor of South Dakota signed a statute making performing abortions illegal, though the law was repealed later that same year in a referendum. In his first few weeks in office, President Obama ended the ban on federal funding for international groups that promote or perform abortions. Known as the global gag rule—introduced by President Reagan in 1984—it prohibited organizations from receiving U.S. aid if they used any of their non-U.S. funding to advocate for or perform abortions.

## Worldwide Abortion Facts

- In 1995, 189 countries adopted the Beijing Platform, which called on governments to deal with unsafe abortions as a major public health concern and to reexamine laws that criminalize women for having illegal abortions.
- In the early twenty-first century abortion on demand is prohibited in seventy-three countries around the world.
- According to the World Health Organization, about 20 million women worldwide have unsafe abortions each year, with 68,000 dying from complications.
- Forty percent of all deaths through unsafe abortions occur in Africa.
- In the United Kingdom, the number of abortions being performed each year has doubled since the 1970s—in 2007 it stood at190,000.[8]
- One in three women in the United Kingdom has an abortion during her lifetime.

- Doctors in the United Kingdom who have a moral objection to abortion are not obliged to perform them, and there are increasing worries that there aren't enough medical staff willing to meet demand.

> I don't sit in judgment. We are here to provide a service. For most women having an abortion is an awful thing to do. No one takes it lightly. You can't deal with contraception without dealing with its failures.
> —Kate Guthrie, a sexual health specialist in the United Kingdom who regularly performs abortions.[9]

## Where Abortion Is Still a Crime

Since 1997 there has been a shift around the world toward liberalizing abortion laws. Countries such as South Africa, Ethiopia, Switzerland, and Cambodia now allow abortion in cases of rape, incest, fetal malformation, and maternal health. In Ireland, which has been the subject of highly controversial test cases, the constitution was amended in 1983 to give the unborn child the same right to life as a mother. Abortion is illegal in Ireland and can only be performed if there is a substantial risk to a mother's life, including suicide. Fetal abnormality is not an acceptable reason for abortion.

What do El Salvador, Malta, Chile, Nicaragua, and Colombia all have in common?

A total ban on abortion. In the case of El Salvador, getting caught can mean a prison sentence of up to thirty years. El Salvador is the only country in the world that has an active law-enforcement apparatus with medical spies, forensic vagina inspectors "who visit the scene of the crime," and police investigators who devote themselves to discovering abortions. Article 1 of El Salvador's Constitution says the government will protect life "from the very moment of conception." The result is that women who want abortions and can afford them fly to Miami, and those who can't resort to back-street practitioners and botched attempts that often end up with the woman in the hospital or dead. Hospital doctors who then have to treat these cases are obliged to report every woman they suspect of having an abortion to the police, or they too can be prosecuted.

This is one woman's abortion story from the capital, San Salvador:

> I came in and was told to lie down. It was not even a bed . . . She came with a piece of cloth and put it underneath my nose, and I felt a little numb. She came back with a long wire, like a TV antenna. It was not like a doctor's instrument. It was just a wire tube with another wire inside it. She put some oil on it and told me to breathe deeply. She put it in. And she was scraping around. I was supposed to be asleep. But I felt pain. I told her it hurt. She said, "Yeah, we're almost done." But she kept scraping around, and I said: "No, no, stop. It's hurting

> me." Then she said, "It's done." She said I would have a fever and I should not go to the doctor or they would report me.[10]

# 4

## Sex

The boundaries between ideas of female beauty and female sexuality have always been blurred and perhaps ought to be recognized as nearly indivisible. Sex and eroticism, idealized fantasies of the perfect female body, pervade society in virtually every area of life and work across the world. It's a complicated, fast-changing arena, and only a few of the subjects related to women and sex are discussed in this section. The particular focus is on areas where ideas of female beauty and eroticism become confused and slip—sometimes hardly noticed—into the more dangerous territory of sadism and extreme sexual violence against women.

### Threadlifts, Skin Peels, and Internal Bras: Images of Beauty

*She has also reportedly had breast implants, a facelift, skin peels, Botox and collagen treatments, viewing cosmetic*

*surgery as vital to upkeeping her famous persona. "If I see
something sagging, bagging and dragging, I'm going to
nip it, tuck it and suck it," she says. "It takes a lot of
money to look this cheap." But unlike most celebrities,
she can laugh about her passion for cosmetic surgery.
Asked if her breasts are real, she responds: "Real big and
real expensive."*

—Interview with Dolly Parton, *Daily Express* 2007

All over the world, bits of women—their faces, hair,
breasts, legs—as well as their entire bodies, are used to
market everything from cars to chocolate bars to cigars.
The cult of celebrity—images of women with pneumatic
breasts and shiny bodies in tiny clothes wearing shoes with
vertiginous heels—has overtaken Western culture to such
a degree that there are very few alternative images of
women in the media at the moment. Large portions of the
world are transfixed by the doings of supermodels, celebrities, and Hollywood stars, and the desire to ape these images of perceived feminine bodily perfection has led to a
burgeoning plastic surgery industry. The latest phenomenon is increasing numbers of girls aged seventeen and
younger who are getting cut and implanted with their first
pair of silicon breasts.

## Plastic Surgery

The word "plastic" comes from the Greek word *plastikos,*
meaning "to mold or shape." As long ago as 700 B.C.

Threadlift: In this new walk-in version of a face lift, the surgeon implants a series of threads through small incisions in the forehead. These threads are tightened, and the loose skin is gathered up, like having a tiny umbrella opened up under the skin.

Liposelection: Similar to liposuction, the technique uses ultrasound to reshape knees, buttocks, and hips. The unwanted fat is liquefied and removed.

Internal bra: The surgeon implants a small piece of gauze or mesh under the skin which lifts the breast so it looks as if the patient is permanently wearing a bra. Another method is to use the patient's own excess skin, which is blasted with a laser and reattached to the breast wall. "Perky" breasts are promised.

Assyrian kings favored surgical nose augmentation—big noses were considered a symbol of power and authority—a very early form of plastic surgery. Modern plastic surgery came out of pioneering work with the burn victims of World War I, when surgeons attempted to reconstruct the severe facial damage they had suffered. There is a now-growing trend for Asian women to go under the knife—in Japan women are having flaps of skin above their eyes removed to make them open wider, so their faces look more Western.[1]

Brazil has the second largest number of cosmetic surgeons in the world—4,000 operate there. Plastic surgery is no longer a taboo subject, and advertisements for the latest procedures are everywhere. Surgeons talk about the "democratization" of plastic surgery, which is no longer the preserve of the rich, and they hope to eventually provide walk-in clinics that everyone can afford.

Women in the West are also using other women's body parts to achieve their own personal ambitions of beauty. They're wearing extensions made from the hair of Indian women who sell it for money to unscrupulous dealers.[2] According to newspaper reports, some of the collagen used for women's lip plumping in the West is extracted from the bodies of executed Chinese prisoners.[3]

## Women and War

*During the battle, which lasted about 50 days, I did not see any women at all. All I knew [was] that as a result of [being without access to women], men's mental condition ends up declining, and that's when I realized once again the necessity of special comfort stations. This desire is the same as hunger or the need to urinate, and soldiers merely thought of comfort stations as practically the same as latrines.*

—Japanese officer, reflecting on the uses of "comfort women" during World War II[4]

*The Government of Japan must provide each of the remedial measures: Recognize and honor the victims and survivors through the creation of memorials, a museum*

*and a library dedicated to their memory and the promise*
*of "never again."*

—One of the twelve recommendations made
by the Women's International War-Crimes
Tribunal on Japan's Military Sexual Slavery
held in Tokyo in December 2000.
The government of Japan declined
to participate.

## Comfort Women

From 1932 until the end of World War II, up to 200,000
so-called comfort women were kept as sexual slaves for the
Japanese Imperial Army. The victims were Chinese, Tai-
wanese, Korean, Filipina, Malaysian, Indonesian, Dutch,
East Timorese, and a few Japanese.

It was an astonishing act of institutionalized cruelty.
The surviving comfort women have now broken their
fifty-year silence, determined to have an apology from
Japan and to make sure no other women have to endure
what they did: they have demanded that these crimes of
sexual violence be redressed. Until 1992, Japan denied
that the system had existed at all, and claimed that the
women involved were all voluntary prostitutes. It is true
that some of the women were already prostitutes, but
once in the camps they were held as prisoners and sexual
commodities. Eighty-six year old Choi Gap-Soon was
taken from Korea when she was fourteen and enslaved for
twelve years:

> Some soldiers were good, others were evil, some kicked and punched me in the face; I lost some teeth. I was kicked in the vagina, and when I refused to serve the soldiers I was beaten by my boss. I worked from nine in the morning until four P.M. serving soldiers; there was always a long queue, waiting soldiers would shout "haiyaku, haiyaku" which means "quickly, quickly." From five P.M. until eight A.M. the second shift began, this was for high-ranking officers who paid more and were allowed to spend the night with women. I had to serve 40 to 50 men per day. I was in extreme pain all the time, it felt like my vagina was on fire.[5]

The first comfort station was set up in Shanghai in 1932, and as the Japanese empire expanded, so did the geographical range of on-site sex for its army—across China, Taiwan, Borneo, the Philippines, many of the Pacific Islands, Singapore, Malaysia, Burma, and Indonesia.

There is conclusive evidence that the comfort women system violated international law at the time—including prohibitions against slavery, war crimes, and crimes against humanity. When the Japanese finally admitted some responsibility in 1992, they failed to issue a full apology for what they did to these women. Former comfort women say they will not stop campaigning until a full apology is made by Japan. The Asian Women's Fund, set up by the Japanese government to distribute "atonement money," is perceived by survivors as a way to buy their silence. Despite growing international pressure, including a resolution

*Comfort woman. Photo courtesy of Amnesty International.*

in 2007 by the European Parliament calling for Japan to recognize its responsibility for comfort women and issue a full apology and compensation, Japan has so far failed to respond.

### Violence against Women as a Weapon of War

Rape is nearly always a component of war and conflict, both for men's sexual gratification and as a means of humiliating the enemy. This has occurred most recently in places like Bosnia, Angola, the Congo, Liberia, and the Darfur region of Sudan (where women and girls have been raped while gathering firewood outside the refugee camps). Girl soldiers who are coerced into rebel militia groups, like the Lord's Resistance Army in Uganda, are treated differently from boys, and are used for sex in the camps instead of, or as well as, fighting. These degraded girls and women may not be used as cannon fodder as the boys are, but they are damaged and mutilated just the same.

The 1949 Geneva Convention on Warfare makes no specific provision regarding women and rape. Article 3 of the convention relates to "persons taking no part in the hostilities," and then goes on to detail a list of acts they are protected from, including "outrages upon personal dignity, in particular, humiliating and degrading treatment."[6] This could be interpreted as including women who have been raped. However, rape has been established as a war crime only since 2002, with the breakthrough Rome

Statute of the International Criminal Court. It cited sexual and gender-based violence as serious crimes under international law, recognizing rape, sexual slavery, trafficking, enforced prostitution, forced pregnancy, enforced sterilization, and any other form of sexual violence as being of comparable gravity with crimes against humanity. The Rome Statute would not have been enacted without the pressure applied by campaigning women's rights groups around the world, including the Women's Caucus for Gender Justice.[7]

### The Democratic Republic of Congo

Raping and abusing women during conflict often means that the victims are ostracized by their communities once the fighting stops. These women are also at risk of being infected with HIV/AIDS, and they may suffer permanent internal injuries. In 2003 Florence was twenty-eight years old, and traveling in a minibus in the Democratic Republic of Congo (DRC) when an armed militia stopped the bus at a roadblock. Florence and five other women were taken to a camp in the forest. There she was raped every day for two months:

> Florence: I fell ill. I was bleeding from my vagina. And the water there smelt really bad. They told me I had an infection.
> *What was the most difficult?*
> F: For me, the most difficult was each time to be raped by so many different soldiers, every day. And then I was almost entirely

" naked throughout that time: I had only my panties. For two months. So I had to use a piece of cloth here [over her breasts] to cover myself.

*Are you married?*

F: My husband threw me out as soon as I got home. Divorced me. For the moment, I'm on my own.

*And in the community? Your neighbourhood?*

F: There's no respect. Every one of them, even if they see you are on the large side, like me, in good health, they say, "But you've got AIDS, you slept with the soldiers." But I'm worried too: I ask myself, perhaps I have got AIDS. And I've deep pains here, in my lower stomach. I couldn't bear to sleep with a man now. It's as if I have wounds inside me. It hurts so much.[8]

## Women and War: Some Statistics

- In the Democratic Republic of Congo 5,000 cases of rape have been recorded in the Uvira area by women's associations since October 2002, corresponding to an average of forty a day.
- In Rwanda between 250,000 and 500,000 women, or about 20 percent of women, were raped during the 1994 genocide.
- In Sierra Leone 94 percent of displaced households surveyed had experienced sexual assaults, including rape, torture, and sexual slavery.

- In Iraq at least 400 women and girls as young as eight were reported to have been raped in Baghdad since April 2003.
- In Bosnia and Herzegovina between 20,000 and 50,000 women were raped during five months of conflict in 1992.
- In some villages in Kosovo, 30 to 50 percent of women of childbearing age were raped by Serbian forces in 1999.[9]

## Women in the Military

*If you're a woman in the military sexual harassment is part of the job.*

—American female soldier[10]

Armies have traditionally been bastions of masculinity, all-male preserves. Women soldiers in the West are often regarded in private as a distraction, at worst a disruption, in war. In 2002 Geoff Hoon, then the British secretary of state for defense, announced that women would continue to be excluded from some direct combat positions. The reasons given were "unit cohesion" and "combat effectiveness"—obfuscating language revealing Hoon's prejudices rather than any facts about women soldiers. More than 16,000 women have served with the U.S. Army in Iraq, Afghanistan, and the Middle East since 2003—that means one in seven soldiers is a woman, and over seventy of them have died in the conflicts. One study reports that

90 percent of women in the U.S. Army have reported incidents of sexual harassment.[11]

Integrating women into a traditionally male military culture has proved very difficult. Even seemingly insignificant things like language can reinforce women's unequal status. Male recruits are often referred to in a derogatory way as "ladies," "girls," "pussies"—meaning they're weak, not proper soldiers. This language contributes to the negative treatment of women. In 2005 the U.S. Army held a review of sexual assaults against women in the military in Iraq. The revelations were shocking, none more so than the testimony of Colonel Janis Karpinski, the former commander of Abu Ghraib prison, as to the causes of death of an unnamed number of soldiers at Camp Victory:

> [W]omen, in fear of getting up in the hours of darkness to go out to the port-a-lets or the latrines were not drinking liquids after 3 or 4 in the afternoon, and in 120 degree heat or warmer, because there was no air-conditioning at most of the facilities, they were dying from dehydration in their sleep. There were no lights near any of their facilities, so women were doubly easy targets in the night.[12]

The women's latrines were situated outside their barracks, and male American soldiers reportedly lay in wait for lone females, to pull them into the latrines and sexually assault and rape them at night.

An independent investigator went to Camp Victory to find out more about the deaths that Colonel Karpinski had reported: "I did indeed find three deaths of women in the year she was talking about attributed to non-hostile causes, which the Army never seems to really explain, so I think it's very possible those are three she was talking about."[13]

In 2006 the British Ministry of Defence found that 99 percent of its 9,384 servicewomen had witnessed "sexualized behavior"—jokes and stories, language and widespread behavior from men they were uncomfortable with on a professional level—in the past year, and that over 50 percent of those who had complained about it said there had been negative consequences for them. The military still has a long, long way to go.[14]

## On the Game: The Sex Industry

*Women had more freedom before the Spanish colonialists, they had freedom in how to exercise their sexuality before the Spanish introduced patriarchal values, made them wear long dresses, taught them that women are second to men, which is reinforced by the teachings of Catholicism which they introduced.*

*—What were the Americans responsible for?*

*They introduced the idea of women being sex objects, the cash economy with these values of the commercialisation of women, the industrialisation of prostitution and so our colonial history has produced a hybrid Filipina. She is expected to be a virgin, she's also expected to*

*be a vamp. A virgin from our feudal patriarchal history
and a vamp because she is expected to be more free sexually, and this was introduced by the American's liberal
attitude.*

—Interview with Lisa Mason,
former secretary general of Gabriella,
a women's shelter in Manila[15]

In the United Kingdom, men spend between £700 million
and £1 billion a year on prostitutes—more than the nation
spends on going to the movies. From the high class prostitutes who cost thousands of dollars a night to the street
walkers who sell sex for a fraction of that, to girls who
work in brothels and for escort agencies, to call girls who
can be called up and ordered like pizza: selling sex is a big
industry, but the women who work in it are marginalized,
treated with contempt, and largely ignored by the rest of
society.

The language surrounding female prostitution is
derogatory and degrading: hookers, whores, slags, sluts.
Women who become prostitutes are more vulnerable to
violence, drug addiction, homelessness, and psychiatric
problems. They tend to fall out of the state safety net, and
their children face a difficult future.

In Britain, where there are three times as many lap-
dancing clubs as rape crisis centers, where female celebrities pole dance for fun, and men's magazines vie with each
other to have the highest "nipple count"—and that's
women's nipples, not men's—the business of paying for

sex has lost much of its stigma. It has become acceptable behavior for men in the West on stag nights to end up in a brothel, where it is becoming increasingly likely that they may be paying for sex with trafficked women. These are women who are often tricked into leaving their home countries, lured by the promise of a legitimate job, who, once they arrive in the United Kingdom (or another country), become virtual prisoners in a brothel, their passports often taken away, and given very small amounts of money for the numbers of men they have to service. Ten years ago, 85 percent of women working in brothels were British citizens; today 85 percent are from outside the United Kingdom. Research published in 2005 showed that the number of British men who admitted using prostitutes doubled between 1995 and 2000: that's one in ten over a lifetime.[16]

## The Legalized Sex Industry: The Netherlands

Those who argue for a worldwide legalized sex industry say that allowing women to work openly in brothels reduces the scope for violence on the street. They say a more transparent prostitution system—where brothels are registered and the women have regular health checks—would also identify and help trafficked women. The Netherlands recognized prostitution as a legal profession in 1988, which means that prostitutes have access to the social security system. They have paid income tax since 1996 and are unionized. However while violence against

*Prostitution on the Achterburgwal in the red light district of Amsterdam.*
*Netherlands, April 2007. © International Labour Organization.*

street walkers has diminished, in the early twenty-first century almost 60 percent of the prostitutes in the Netherlands are foreign nationals, and the country has some of the highest numbers of trafficked women in Europe. Amsterdam's 5,000 sex workers—with the famous window prostitutes of De Wallen red-light district—mean the city has become a destination for sex tourism. There is also the counter-argument that a legalized sex industry legitimizes men's use of prostitutes, and allows men to justify their actions because the government ostensibly condones it and says it's okay to buy sex.

Campaigners and women's activists have debated how to solve the problem of prostitution, especially acute with the large numbers of trafficked women in the first decade of the twenty-first century. There are two camps for the arguments surrounding the sex trade:

---

### For and Against

Prostitution is eradicable:

> Why do we have to accept prostitution? Yes, it has been with us for a long time, but so have poverty and racism. We do not hear governments declaring that "racism is here to stay."
>
> —Julie Bindel, founder of
> Justice for Women

> Prostitution is here forever:
>
> In a world with no poverty, no inequality, no violence and universal sexual contentment within relationships, prostitution would wither. Until that utopian day arrives, sex for sale will remain with us. It thrives in imperfect, liberal societies such as ours, it existed during the time of the Taleban in Afghanistan, and it flourishes in plenty of political systems in between.
>
> —Diane Taylor, magazine editor for Mainliners, a U.K. charity that works with drug users and sex workers[17]

## Where Men Are Criminalized: Sweden

In 1999, Sweden passed legislation that decriminalized the selling of sex. In other words, the men using prostitutes became the criminals, the women their victims. It is the only country to have taken this step. The Swedish law says:

> In Sweden, prostitution is regarded as an aspect of male violence against women and children. It is officially acknowledged as a form of exploitation of women and children and constitutes a significant social problem . . . gender equality will remain unattainable so long as men buy, sell and exploit women and children by prostituting them.

When Sweden passed this groundbreaking legislation, nearly 50 percent of the members of parliament were women. After initial resistance and extensive retraining of police and law enforcers, the number of men seeking sex has dropped by 80 percent, and the number of women on the street is down by two-thirds. The evidence is that criminalizing prostitution in this way has also dramatically cut down the trafficking of women into Sweden by organized crime gangs. However, detractors say that hidden commercial sex has increased as a result, as has sex for sale on the Internet, and that the most socially marginalized women, those who work on the street, have suffered most.[18]

## "Girls A-Go-Go"—a bar in Thailand

Since 1960, prostitution has technically been illegal in Thailand, but this prohibition was circumvented by the Entertainment Places Act passed the following year, which makes it possible for massage parlors, bars, night-clubs, and tea houses to operate as de facto brothels. The Thai government passed the act in an effort to increase state revenue from the illegal sex industry—in effect the government is profiting from women's sex work. However, because it is still an officially unacknowledged industry, the women themselves receive no legal or health protection in return.

## Self-protection in Sonagachi, India

The Sonagachi project is a movement of sex workers in Sonagachi, the largest red-light district of Kolkata (formerly Calcutta), who are successfully negotiating safer sex relationships with clients as well as better treatment from society at large, including the police. A quarter of the managerial positions in Sonagachi are reserved for sex workers. They decide what actions to take, such as setting up health clinics for sex workers or distributing free condoms. The project, led by the prostitutes themselves, is giving power to women at the bottom of Indian society.

## X-rated

*Right now it's still in my mind. But I've been musing at what I would do if I could make a 3D porn film! It hasn't been green-lit yet, as I still have a few things to work out on it!*

—Director Quentin Tarantino, on his
future plans for women in his films,
speaking after the release of *Death Proof,*
his exploitation film in the *Grindhouse*
double bill project.[19]

### Women and Porn

Pornography is the explicit description or portrayal of sex in any media—films, books, animation, photographs, video games, etc.—that is trying to stimulate an erotic response in the reader or viewer. Porn is treated very differently from mainstream descriptions of sex, and porn stars—male or female—seldom cross over into the mainstream celebrity world. Although the men and women who take part in pornography may do so voluntarily, the argument is that the very existence, and increasingly easy availability of hard-core pornography, degrades all women.

The Internet has made it possible for the porn industry to go global—it's no longer a case of smuggling illegal videos through customs. Now anyone can download whatever they like from all over the world at any time. It's almost impossible to regulate the Internet porn industry; instead of magazines under the bed or on the top shelf of the newsstand, the Internet provides porn on tap everywhere, all the time. Laws vary all over the world, but in the United Kingdom it is not illegal to look at porn online unless it involves children. The proliferation of sex sites on the Internet has made accidental viewing of porn, particularly by children, a major hazard when they're surfing. Many people, not just anti-porn campaigners, believe that Western society has become desensitized to porn because we are constantly surrounded by sexualized and erotic images of women in advertising. In the United Kingdom, every day for almost forty years *The Sun*—which has the highest circulation of any English-language newspaper in the world—has run a full-page photograph of a topless woman on page three. Degrading images of women are part of our everyday life, and a survey in 2009 of 400 schoolboys aged between fourteen and seventeen in the United Kingdom revealed that three out of ten boys say they learn about sex from porn, and that the average teenage boy watches ninety minutes of porn a week. Their viewing includes bestiality, group sex, and lesbian intercourse. "Porn," says one boy, "is everywhere." The hardcore nature of online porn and its child abuse content is increasing to meet an apparently insatiable demand for new images. An Internet watchdog reported in 2007 that images depicting penetrative and sadistic sex on the Internet had quadrupled in the last three years. On pedophile sites, 80 percent of the children used are female and 91 percent appear to be under twelve years old. Nearly 90 percent of these sites—which number over 3,000—are hosted in the United States and Russia.[20]

## Gorno: A New Low for Misogyny

There has been a resurgence of misogynist violence and pornography in films aimed at the mainstream cinema. The director Eli Roth justified the choice of poster advertising his 2007 film *Hostel Part II*—which shows some glistening raw meat—in the following way:

> Any time people see women in a horror film, they say, "Oh, these girls are just pieces of meat." And literally, in *Hostel Part II,* that's exactly what they are. They are the bait, they are the meat, they are the grist for the mill. So I thought it was actually a really smart poster . . . and really, really disgusting! I love it.[21]

This genre of horror film is so violent, degrading, and dehumanizing to women that it's being called "gorno," which is a conflation of the words "gore" and "porn," extreme violence and sex. Women are portrayed as just sexual commodities, prey to men's most violent sexual and sadistic fantasies. For the release of *Grindhouse* in 2007, a doll called "Rapist Number One," modeled on Quentin Tarantino's character in "Planet Terror," was created as part of the merchandising tie-in. Violent computer games, such as Grand Theft Auto, normalize the view of women as the ultimate victims to be controlled or abused by men.

### Real-life Gorno

Off screen, sex and violence merge for real in the fate of trafficked women, abducted and forced into sex work abroad. Trafficking—modern-day slavery—is one of the fastest growing international crimes in Europe. Women from all over eastern Europe and the former Soviet Union are becoming just another commodity in the marketplace. Even if they manage to escape and return home they are faced with the same problems of poverty and debt, as well as the stigma of having been trafficked and thus the shame they bring on their families, who often then reject them.

One day, in 2005, a fourteen-year-old Moldovan girl named Galina and her friend Irina accepted a lift home to their village from two boys parked in a car outside their school. A few days later, despite having no passports, after train journeys across three national borders where border guards were bribed to turn a blind eye, Galina and Irina's kidnappers left the girls in an apartment in Moscow, thousands of miles from home, with no papers or money.

---

**Interview with Galina**

---

You know we wanted to run away but the apartment we were locked in was on the fifth floor and so we couldn't jump, it was too high, there was no telephone. *Did you know what was going to happen, had you heard of the same thing happening to other girls?*

When we were in the train we understood what was going on, and the woman told us she's taking us to Moscow to work there. We tried to run away from the train at one of the stations but we were caught and Irina was beaten severely, and that's how we failed to escape from the train. *What happened to you in Moscow?*

We stayed in the apartment for two days, and then we were beaten and they said you are going to work, so in two days we went to work. *Working with men?*

Yes.[22]

---

Highly prized as a virgin, Galina was sold for hundreds of dollars. On her first night the man who had bought her raped her, hung her by her feet from a sixth floor balcony window, and mutilated her genitals with a knife. Six months later, with incredible courage, Galina managed to escape the apartment and make her way back to Moldova. She is one of the lucky few who is being looked after in the only women's shelter in the capital, Chisinau. Galina has had to have many operations to correct the internal damage done while in captivity, and she is being helped to start her life again and train as a hairdresser.

Moldova, a small land-locked country between Ukraine and Romania, has one of the highest rates of trafficked women in the world; an estimated 1 million women are currently outside the country working as prostitutes. Some women and girls like Galina are kidnapped and taken abroad; others voluntarily sign up with foreign employment agencies and are promised jobs as waitresses, dancers, or nannies. Some of these are genuine jobs, but the majority of women find themselves forced into sex work instead. Interestingly, some of the women who have escaped said they knew full well that they were going abroad for sex work, but they thought the risk was worth it for the money due to the utter lack of any other options at home, and believed that they could stay in control and manage their own lives. What they hadn't bargained for was the violence of the traffickers, coupled with their virtual imprisonment once their passports and money had been taken away.

## Protecting Women

There are new initiatives in Moldova that are starting to address the tragedy of trafficking. Since 2006, no child (male or female) under the age of eighteen has been able to leave the country alone. They have to travel with their parents, or with a letter from their parents giving permission for someone else to take on the responsibility. The rehabilitative women's shelter in Chisinau is small, but nevertheless it exists, with psychiatric help on hand. There is also a twenty-four-hour hotline for parents and friends who are worried about missing girls and women. Lucas Moodysson's award-winning 2002 film, *Lilya 4-Ever,* a powerful depiction of a young Russian girl's slide into sexual slavery, is being used as part of antitrafficking public education campaign in Moldova and elsewhere in Eastern Europe.

The international community has also introduced measures to curb the trafficking epidemic. In 2002 the United Nations adopted the Protocol to Prevent, Suppress, and Punish Trafficking in Persons, and this was strengthened three years later when the Council of Europe made protection and assistance of trafficked persons a requirement rather than a recommendation.

# 5

## Poverty

*Women do two-thirds of the world's work, receive 10 percent of the world's income and own 1 percent of the means of production.*

—Richard H. Robbins[1]

Poverty is one of the most endemic and inescapable problems that women face; two out of every three adults living in poverty in the world are women. The ways that women become poverty-stricken are often specifically related to their gender, such as being widowed, having fewer opportunities for paid employment than men, or having casual, erratic employment, which results in having no pension and no job security. The work that the majority of women do—caring for their children and home—is largely unrecognized and unpaid. Poverty is also often the result of domestic violence and of being forced to flee the family home to find refuge. Restrictions on property ownership, inheritance laws favoring men and sons, and lack of access to economic resources—such as credit—also discriminate against women and drive them into poverty. This section looks at just a few of the ways poverty disproportionately affects women worldwide.

## Environment and Gender

*Advancing gender equality . . . may also be one of the best ways of saving the environment, and countering the dangers of overcrowding and other adversities associated with population pressure. The voice of women is critically important for the world's future—not just for women's future.*

—Nobel Prize–winning economist
Amartya Sen[2]

Understanding the relationship between gender and the environment, especially for women living in poverty, is crucial to coping with future environmental challenges, including climate change. Women are often on the front line of dealing with environmental degradation, especially in the developing world, because there they are predominantly responsible for subsistence agriculture, for finding sources of water and firewood, and for sustaining the family and the community. Women account for 51 percent of the world's agricultural workforce—they put in hard physical labor in the fields in order to grow vegetables, fruit, and grain for their families, and also to earn extra cash. In Southeast Asia, women provide 90 percent of the labor needed for rice cultivation. Women's vital contributions and their knowledge of their environment are often de-valued and ignored by men.

## The Effects of Environmental Degradation for Women

- Deforestation increases the time women have to spend doing their traditional tasks of seeking wood for fuel or safe, clean water. In the Indian state of Gujarat, women now spend four or five hours a day collecting wood, whereas previously they only needed to go out once every four or five days.[3]
- Soil erosion, floods, water shortages, and crop failures all mean poor harvests; small and over-used through necessity, household gardens are usually tended by women in the developing world.
- Women's social realities and biological needs bring them closer than men to environmental hazards. Women are the ones often fetching the contaminated water, and exposure to toxic chemicals and pesticides through drinking water or pollution can cause health problems. These can result in birth defects for their children, or the problems are passed onto babies through breast milk. In China's Gansu province, discharges from a fertilizer factory are thought to have caused a high number of still-births and miscarriages in the region.[4]

## Giving Women the Tools

Education about sustainable development, management of land resources, implementation of antidesertification measures, and general survival strategies are essential for women to be able to make the best use of their land. If women are taught how to farm responsibly and for the long-term good of the land, they can rise to the challenge. A World Bank study in Ghana found that women's plots had a lower rate of decline in soil fertility than did men's—even within the same household.[5] Women who subsistence farm single-handedly in Africa and elsewhere are generally given the worst plots of land to farm and are denied access to tools until after the men have finished with them. Consequently, they often miss the right times and opportunities for planting and harvesting and therefore have to work harder to get a good crop. They also have to rely on help from their children and neighbors.

Farming is different all over the world, and changes to historical norms in the industry are emerging all the time. In Britain, traditional farming has always been male dominated. However, with the rise of organic farming in the last two decades, the ratio of male to female organic farmers is fifty-fifty.

## Natural Disasters

*When the survivors of Lampu'uk had picked themselves up out of the mud of the tsunami, several appalling facts*

*became clear. The first was that their town no longer ex-*
*isted. The second was that four out of five of its former*
*inhabitants were dead. But it took a while to realise the*
*strangest thing of all: that among those who made it to*
*higher ground, or who kept their heads above the surging*
*waters, so few were women.*[6]

The South Asian tsunami of December 26, 2004, hit women hardest, as is so often the case with natural disasters. There were various reasons for this: women tried to help older relatives or children as well as themselves to escape, many more men than women can swim in that region, and men are far more used to climbing trees than are women. Even women who could swim were weighed down by their children clinging to them in the waves, so there was a smaller chance of either surviving.

On India's southeast coast, women traditionally play a major role in the fishing industry, processing the fish the men bring in. On that December morning the women were all lined up, waiting on the shoreline as usual for the boats to come back, when the waves hit and the women took the brunt of their force. Across the Palk Strait in Sri Lanka, the waves arrived in the eastern town of Batticaloa at the time when the men were not around because the women were taking their Sunday bathe in the sea. Farther around the coast, in the busy market town of Hambantota, women were sitting on the ground in the marketplace in their saris, surrounded by the fruit and vegetables they were selling. They died because their saris got soaked and became heavy and waterlogged. They didn't hitch them up or strip them off—in that culture a woman does not show her knees in public, even to save her life.

Natural disasters can never be prevented, but their disproportionate impact on women can be lessened through education of both sexes. Through Nobel Prize–winning Kenyan environmentalist Wangari Maathai's Green Belt Movement, poor women have planted more than 30 million trees on farms, schools, and church compounds throughout Africa. Trees are vital in preventing or ameliorating the effects of natural disasters such as landslides during floods, and the mangrove swamps surrounding the Maldives archipelago saved the islands during the tsunami. Maathai sees the movement as a women-led social and ecological transformation:

> It took me a lot of days and nights to convince people that women could improve their environment without much technology or without much financial resources.[7]

## Globalization

*Economic systems which value profits often do so at the expense of female labor.*

Radhika Coomaraswamy, Under-Secretary-General, Special Representative for Children and Armed Conflict[8]

*Women are seen, and hence favoured, as a passive, compliant, temporary workforce that will accept low wages without demanding labour and human rights.*

—Christine Chinkin,
"International Law and Policy"[9]

Christine Chinkin, an expert on international women's rights, argues that globalization has brought about a weakening of state power throughout the developing world. Countries are unwilling to discourage foreign investment because they want to reap the benefits of globalization, but the consequence is often a relaxation of internal economic and labor laws. As women are often the key workers in the kinds of jobs that foreign investment brings, it is often women who pay the price for profits of globalization that men and male-dominated societies enjoy. Women's work is of low economic value, and women have little or no job security or protected working conditions. Often these working women are economic migrants, which makes them doubly vulnerable to exploitation.

## Textiles—Globalization's Success Story?

Women in the textile industry in places like Bangladesh, Sri Lanka, the Philippines, Mexico, and Guatemala, which supply cheap clothes to the rest of the world, are being offered jobs in preference to men. Dinesh Hinduja, who owns Gokaldas Exports, one of India's most successful garment

*Textile factory worker, Sudan.* © *International Labour Organization.*

companies, explains why the majority of his workforce of 33,000 are women:

> We try not to hire men; they are less reliable. We had one man who was a drunkard and we fired him. He appealed and it took us fifteen years and huge amounts of management time before we won the appeal.[10]

Compliant, hard working, grateful for employment, and unlikely to make a fuss if they are fired—that's why women are generally preferred to men in this part of the globalized marketplace.

There are an estimated 1.5 million textile workers in Bangladesh; this industry is the country's biggest exporter, contributing 76 percent of the total export earnings. The

NGO War on Want reports that 80 percent of Bangladesh's workforce are women between the ages of fourteen and twenty-nine who, as unskilled workers, earn about fourteen dollars a month. The average minimum monthly wage in Bangladesh is twenty dollars. These women are often subject to dangerous working conditions and long hours—sometimes forced to work up to sixteen hours a day or through the night to complete an order—and they may not get paid until months later. The women usually live in hostels near the factories, and they are in danger of being raped and attacked going to and from work at late hours. Employers often prevent them from forming unions, which is a denial of their basic rights according to the International Labour Organization (ILO). Human rights organizations consider these women to be an exploited work force, and agencies like the National Garment Workers Federation are trying to give them the tools to improve their own lives by educating them about their rights.[11]

## The Effects of Globalization on Women

- Increased migration: moving from rural to urban areas to find work is a result of globalization. In cases where men leave their families to find work, the women are left on their own, struggling to bring up children and caring for older relations. When their husbands return, there's the risk they'll infect their wives with sexually transmitted diseases picked up away from home. Sometimes the husbands never return, and leave their families. In the most extreme cases, mothers are forced to abandon their children to find work.

- Economic liberalization: the relaxing of borders that has accompanied globalization has led to an increase in transnational crime, particularly in the trafficking of women.

- The Internet: in many parts of the world, women are far less likely than men to own or control access to the Internet. This means they are missing out on the benefits of globalization through lack of knowledge about or access to information technology.

The poorest all over the world are missing out most on the benefits of globalization, and two out of every three of the world's adults living in poverty are women.

### Is Globalization All Bad for Women?

These new jobs have brought a degree of independence that has opened up women's life opportunities. Now there is the possibility of helping their families financially, paying for education, building a house, and assisting relatives in need. Women have also gained the freedom that comes with being a migrant worker and perhaps escaping from the cultural and religious strictures of their homes. However, these benefits must all be framed within the problems of globalization and the need to legislate for women's rights within this new, rapidly changing world.

Initiatives such as microcredit are taking on the negative impact of globalization for women and turning it around, offering a viable economic reality through self-employment and empowerment in the wider community.

Muhammad Yunus had the idea of lending small amounts of money to a group of families in Bangladesh after the terrible famine there of 1974. This grew into the Grameen Bank, which specializes in microfinance, typically lending less than $100 at a time to the poor to help them escape the cycle of debt and subsistence living. The Grameen Bank now has more than 7 million borrowers, of

*A woman in Valle, Honduras sets up a street storefront to sell household items. She has built her business with the help of microcredit loans. UN photo/Mark Garten.*

whom 97 percent are women. The bank has 2,468 branches covering over 80,000 villages in Bangladesh with an exemplary loan recovery rate of over 98 percent. More than half of the borrowers have risen out of acute poverty, and are now able to send their children to school, eat three meals a day, and have access to clean drinking water, a sanitary toilet, and a rainproof house. This system of microcredit is now the basis for similar banks in over forty-three countries—with women leading the way out of poverty for their families.

Selina, who lives in rural Bangladesh, is eighteen and has two children. As a child of seven she began to work because her parents were unable to support her. She had an arranged marriage when she was twelve, and her parents sold their land to pay for her dowry. She borrowed sixty dollars from the Grameen bank to start a small business and to enable her to improve her life and plan ahead for expenses like birth control, housing, her children's education.

Women have been able to take responsibility and control of their future through economic independence. However, this new autonomy has had repercussions from some men in the communities who have felt threatened by their wives' new confidence and access to the public space. The United Nations Development Fund for Women (UNIFEM) has reported cases of verbal and physical aggression directed against women microcredit users. Other studies in Bangladesh point out that women are still at risk of losing control of the loans to male relatives if they are excluded from participating in markets outside their homes to buy and sell their goods.

Nevertheless, in a fast-changing world, microcredit is offering some of the poorest women in the world a chance to break their cycle of poverty and giving them the potential to operate in a wider, globalized market.

## Women Refugees

*Had that group [of women] stood out in some way— visually or physically, because of their ethnic background, or a religious difference, or whatever—we would have made sure they got food. But because they were women, it didn't even occur to us. It didn't even occur to me, I have to admit—to my shame.*

—John Telford, UNHCR (United Nations
High Commissioner for Refugees)
emergency officer, remembering the flood
of Kurdish refugees leaving Iraq in 1991.
All the food marshals were men,
and little aid reached any women.[12]

In any civilian exodus, women and children normally make up three-quarters of the refugee population; they are also the poorest of the refugees. However, prevailing attitudes and cultural expectations mean that women have fewer opportunities than men to have their voices heard, to fight for their share of aid, or to have their asylum applications processed successfully. They are called the "invisible refugees."

## The Scale of the Problem

The office of the United Nations High Commissioner for Refugees (UNHCR) reported that at the start of 2006 there were 20.8 million people "of concern" to the agency around the world. Nearly 9 percent of these are refugees, who have fled across national borders in order to escape war or violence at home. They cannot return, and they qualify as refugees according to the 1951 Geneva Convention "owing to a well-founded fear of persecution because of their race, religion, nationality, political opinion or membership of a particular social group." They usually then seek asylum, which is the right to be recognized as "bona fide refugees and receive legal protection and material assistance." There are around 750,000 asylum seekers whose claims have not yet been processed. More than half of these claims were lodged in Europe.

## Worse for Women

Female refugees, sometimes very young and perhaps illiterate, can become responsible overnight for protecting and feeding their entire family. Fleeing from conflict or disaster, they often leave behind their husbands, as well as their homes and livelihoods. Aid workers and field operators who work with women in refugee camps need to have training in gender awareness and cultural sensitivity to avoid discriminating against women. UNHCR gives an example of a male aid worker handing out supplies of sanitary napkins to girls in front of their male classmates in an African school. The girls were mortified.

There is also the problem of aid workers bringing their own cultural bias to the refugee camps:

> One field supervisor refused to introduce a schooling program in one Middle Eastern country with the argument that educated women would find it difficult to get married and the comment that "I certainly wouldn't marry such a woman myself."[13]

Women in the camps—supposedly a place of safety for them—are vulnerable to rape and physical violence. There have been instances where going to the toilet or collecting firewood and water in a big refugee camp and its immediate vicinity becomes dangerous for women. Aid workers need to be aware of this and take steps to prevent it. In some Kenyan refugee camps, Somali women were repeatedly sexually attacked until the camp layout was reorganized and lighting was improved in an effort to stop the attackers.

> In 1981 when 452 boats arrived in Thailand carrying 15,479 refugees, UNHCR's statistics were a study of horror: 349 boats had been attacked an average of three times each; 578 women were raped, 228 women were abducted and 881 people were dead or missing.[14]

## What Makes a Refugee?

In the United Kingdom, refugee women's legal groups have lobbied to develop guidelines for gender in asylum cases.[15] These guidelines address some of the difficulties that women asylum-seekers face, including not being given female interpreters and having to describe details of sexual abuse or rape in front of men, which means that often they won't tell their full stories. Being interviewed along with their husbands and children may also constrain them. These guidelines, although somewhat diluted in content, were finally adopted by the Home Office in 2004 but were never made mandatory. The Home Office recognized that decisions over refugee status had been biased in the past. Two years later, research by Asylum Aid showed that these guidelines were still not being followed properly—interviewers had little knowledge about the women's countries of origin, were not giving women's claims enough time, and were not adequately recognizing that "persecution" in the conventional sense does not always correspond to women's actual experiences.

## Failed Refugees

Two-thirds of asylum applications end in failure in the United Kingdom, which means that after twenty-one days that person is expected to return to his or her own country. All financial support and state benefits are usually cut off, including free health care at National Health Service hospitals, even for pregnant women unless it's an emergency. If they are unable to return home for whatever reason, these failed asylum seekers often fall into destitution. There are reports of some of these women ending up on the street, turning to prostitution in order to survive, and being given somewhere to sleep in return for sex.[16] This is called transactional, or survival, sex and it happens all over the world.

## Returning Home Again

Most refugees want to go home again once the conflict has ended, but returnees, as they're called, face new problems in resettling. Women especially often come up against the same obstacles that they did in the camps. In southern Sudan, about one million voluntary returnees have come home since the peace agreement was signed in 2004 after over twenty years of civil war, trusting and hoping that the current situation in Darfur will not spill over and destabilize their fragile peace again.

The education system in Sudan has suffered catastrophically as a result of the conflict. Southern Sudan's literacy rates are amongst the worst in the world, and girl returnees are the worst affected. The situation is exacerbated by the lack of female teachers in the region to act as role models for the girls and to encourage them to take their education seriously. UNHCR established a teacher-training college in the Kenyan Kakuma refugee camp for southern Sudanese refugees while they were there, but only

10 out of the 211 recent graduates from Kakuma were women. Trying to redress this problem, the new government of southern Sudan has written into its postconflict constitution an affirmative action clause that reserves 25 percent of its government positions for women. This quota cannot yet be filled, but it's hoped that it will act as an incentive to keep girls in school, and that in the future they will enter government and the civil service.[17]

### Victims and Spectators

*Fifteen years ago, refugee women were viewed through a one-dimensional lens—as a mother. We did not see them as "complete women"—complicated human beings with an array of potential problems, not just childbirth. We have moved on from there in our attitude toward women and such problems as sexual violence or genital mutilation. There has been progress.*

—Serge Malé, senior epidemiologist
with UNHCR

Increasingly, the importance of training and equipping women and girl children while they live in refugee camps is being reassessed. The goal is to empower them to change their futures by providing food and shelter, giving them leadership, education, and economic skills, and ceasing to treat women as victims—all of which will help them to start up small businesses and get involved in camp administration.

" When you are looking for leaders, look to us. Do not think that because women wear a veil, we do not have a voice. I have often heard that Afghan women are not political; that peace and security is a man's work. I am here to challenge that illusion. For the last 20 years of my life, the leadership of men has only brought war and suffering.

—Jamila, an Afghan refugee, speaking to the UN Security Council

# 6

# Making
# Changes

Historically, change and progress for women in all areas of life and work—education, health, politics—are often accomplished through the law. Very few lasting or meaningful changes in women's rights can be achieved without a legal framework to back them up. This section looks at how progress is underpinned by national and international legislation, and how and when these laws have been pushed through by individuals and groups campaigning for reform. Sometimes significant legal changes in seemingly unrelated areas—such as peacekeeping or sport—can have a dramatic effect on how women are viewed in society, which in turn promotes further changes in the law to support women's rights.

## Activism

*He touched me . . . that's when I kicked him in a very bad place.*

—Irene Morgan Kirkaldy in an interview
with the *Washington Post* in 2000

Irene Morgan (later known as Irene Morgan Kirkaldy) was returning to her home in Maryland from Virginia on a Greyhound bus in July 1944 after visiting her mother. The bus became crowded, and the driver told her to move to the back and give up her seat for a white person. She refused, and when a sheriff's deputy boarded the bus and tried to twist her arm, she kicked him. Later, Irene Morgan pleaded guilty to resisting arrest and paid a $100 fine, but she refused to pay an additional $10 fine for violating a Virginia law on segregated seating on public transport. She appealed, and a team of lawyers from the NAACP (National Association for the Advancement of Colored People), including a young black lawyer named Thurgood Marshall, took her case to the Supreme Court. They won, arguing that the Virginia law was unconstitutional and threatened free movement across state lines. In 1967 Thurgood Marshall become the first African-American justice of the U.S. Supreme Court.

When President Bill Clinton awarded Irene Morgan Kirkaldy the Presidential Citizens Medal in 2001, the citation read: "When Irene Morgan boarded a bus for Baltimore in the summer of 1944, she took the first step on a journey that would change America forever."[1]

Just over a decade later, in Montgomery, Alabama, in 1955, Rosa Parks also refused to give up her seat for a white man, and she was also arrested. The actions of both women triggered the beginning of the civil rights movement in America.

## The Feminist Movement in the United States

Women's participation early in the American civil rights movement of the mid-twentieth century led to the feminist activism of the seventies and eighties. In 1963 the American writer Betty Friedan published *The Feminine Mystique,* in which she described the boredom and dissatisfaction of middle-class American housewives in a way that had not been publicly discussed before. The book became a huge success, and is said by some to have initiated the modern women's rights movement. In the same year, the United States Congress passed the Equal Pay Act, which made it illegal for women to be paid less than men in the same job. The 1964 Civil Rights Act was a landmark piece of legislation prohibiting racial discrimination in either education or the workplace; it included a late amendment on sex-discrimination as well.

In the early 1970s like-minded women gradually organized into a network of women's groups, fighting for equal rights and campaigning against rape, pornography, and gender-based violence. They criticized male-dominated aspects of society and sexist attitudes and language. These feminists were widely derided by society, which lampooned them for what they wore, for their supposedly man-hating attitudes, and for their rejection of so-called normal family values. Despite this, the women's movement made progress in changing the public perception of women and what they were capable of achieving. There are still plenty of issues to be fought over; for instance, there is no such thing as paid maternity leave required by law in America, in contrast with the generous provision in the majority of western European countries, especially Scandinavia. In Sweden, for example, all working parents are entitled to sixteen months paid leave per child.

## Fighting for Change around the World

> *It is incredible how the organized gangs of criminals and the clandestine groups continue to operate with complete impunity. It is shocking to see such ineffectiveness and lack of political will to confront these evils and apply justice. We are sick of speeches. These are human beings, Guatemalans of flesh and blood who continue to be the victims of violence, intolerance and the hidden, parallel powers.*

Outspoken words like these have brought regular intimidation and death threats to Marielos Monzon, a campaigning journalist who presents a morning radio program from Guatemala City's Radio Universidad exposing human rights violations.

News anchor and civil rights activist Rania al-Baz caused huge controversy in Saudi Arabia when, in 2004, she allowed pictures of her very disfigured face to be published after her husband had beaten her almost to death. She had thirteen facial fractures, and had to undergo extensive reconstructive surgery. With the publication of this

*Marielos Monzon. Photo courtesy of Amnesty International.*

photo, she breached the taboo in Saudi Arabia of keeping domestic violence secret. Eventually her husband gave himself up to the police and received a six-month prison sentence and 300 lashes. Rania continues to fight for women's rights in the only country in the world where women are prohibited from driving, even in an emergency.

New technology is bringing new freedoms to women, particularly in the Middle East. In Egypt, the demographics of bloggers are changing as the numbers grow. The profile of a typical blogger used to be a male university graduate in his mid-twenties, but now it's more likely to be an eighteen- or nineteen-year-old female student.[2] This picture is being repeated all over the Middle East and beyond:

> " Thanks to the Internet, Web sites and Weblogs, new bridges between Iranian women in the diaspora and those inside Iran are built and old ones are strengthened on a regular basis . . . Perhaps nobody sees us, but we exist and we exert our mark in the world around us. I assure you that if you look around carefully, you shall see our tracks.
>
> —Shadi Sadr, Iranian journalist, activist, and lawyer, 2004

The last two decades have also seen activism in a few men's groups across the world—pioneering movements that aim to re-educate society about what are and are not acceptable ways to treat women:

> If it were between countries, we'd call it a war. If it were a disease, we'd call it an epidemic. If it were an oil spill, we'd call it a disaster. But it's happening to women, and it's just an everyday affair. It is violence against women. It is sexual harassment at work and sexual abuse of the young. It is the beating or the blow that millions of women suffer each and every day. It is rape at home and on dates. It is murder.

These are the words of Michael Kaufman, cofounder of the White Ribbon Campaign in Canada, which he started in 1991 following the massacre in Montreal of fourteen women engineering students two years earlier. Men who participate in the White Ribbon Campaign have to make three personal pledges:

- Never to commit violence against women;
- Never to condone violence against women;
- Never to remain silent about violence against women.

White Ribbon works to educate men in schools, universities, corporations, and labor unions; there are now campaigning groups in over fifty countries.

CORIAC, or the Collective of Men for Egalitarian Relationships, was founded in Mexico in 1993 to give men space to examine their violent feelings toward women, to self-educate, and to learn to express their anger and frustration in nonviolent ways. CORIAC and the

White Ribbon Campaign are examples of progressive initiatives that aim to change the way men and women coexist in relationships and to work toward a more egalitarian society.

## Keeping the Peace

*We declare the doctrine that war is inevitable to be both a denial of the sovereignty of reason and a betrayal of the deepest instincts of the human heart. With a sense of our share in the failure to prevent the wars of the past and of the present and in sorrow for the suffering, the desolate and the oppressed, we, the members of this Congress, urge the women of all nations to work for their own enfranchisement and unceasingly to strive for a just and lasting peace.*

On April 28, 1915, these words were part of the resolution agreed to by a group of women who met in the Netherlands at the International Congress of Women to protest against the First World War then devastating Europe. The women who met were prominent in the International Suffrage Alliance and saw the connection between their struggle for equality and the struggle for peace. They later became the Women's International League for Peace and Freedom.

Women don't usually make wars, and they don't usually make the peace either. The role of women when societies and communities collapse is crucial—from caring for their children and older relations to coping with displacement, lack of food, disruption, and violence.

## Women Waging Peace in Sierra Leone

Throughout the war in Sierra Leone, which lasted from 1991 to 2002, women from all ethnic groups and classes were active in holding rallies and marches, educating people, and calling for peace and justice. Unusually, women fought in this conflict, and they were also crucial in ending it and bringing about both a formal and an informal peace process. In the first peace negotiations—called the Lomé process—two women from each side of the conflict were among the delegates, and consequently certain gender-specific elements were put into the final document. For instance, Article 28 called for special attention to victimized women and girls in formulating rehabilitation, reconstruction, and development programs. When the Lomé Peace Accord collapsed and the ceasefire was breached, it was groups of women who took to the streets shouting, "Not again, enough is enough!"

Women's activism in Sierra Leone reached its peak in 2000 when a group of elderly women representing churches and mosques demanded a meeting with the rebel leader Foday Sankoh in the capital, Freetown. At his office the women were turned away and treated roughly, verbally abused by his guards and advisors. In protest against this treatment, the women hitched up their skirts, bent over, and exposed themselves. When word got out about this, the population was shocked, but also mobilized because what these women had done represented a great insult to Sankoh; they had eroded his power and the cult of personality surrounding him. The mass demonstrations that followed on May 8, 2000, marked a turning part in the conflict.[3]

## When Peace Goes Wrong

The under-representation of women's views in judicial processes is one reason why crimes against women are prone to be unrecorded and unaddressed in a peace deal. The reconstruction phase after a war or conflict, when elections are being held and the government and constitution are being formed, is a crucial period for women to have a say and make a difference to society.[4] However, in the past, women have rarely been consulted about acceptable means of seeking justice. This means that, oftentimes, impunity for violence against women is the weak link in legal frameworks for reconstruction. In the Democratic Republic of Congo, one woman activist complained, "Large numbers of atrocities have been committed during the war here, but even now there is no justice. We cannot go to local authorities, as they have no power."[5]

When Dr. Massouda Jalal ran for president of Afghanistan in 2004 she said, "I can win on 9 October because I am a woman, and in Afghanistan it is only women who have no blood on their hands." She didn't win—Hamid Karzai did—but her attempt became a symbol of hope for women in the reconstruction of civil society in Afghanistan. She was appointed, predictably enough, to be minister for women's affairs and is working to rebuild a society where her daughters can achieve as much as her sons. "The new Afghanistan should be built by the hand of a mother," she says.

## Peace Activism

In August 1981 a group of thirty-six women in the United Kingdom walked from Cardiff to a then little-known Royal Air Force station in Berkshire called Greenham Common, to protest against U.S. cruise missiles being stored there. They set up a women-only camp around the perimeter fence, and staged "actions" in which they pushed paper doves or baby clothes through the fence. At one point, 50,000 women gathered on the Common to join hands around the fence. Confrontations with the police were often heated and resulted in hundreds of arrests over the years. Although the missiles were removed from the base in the early 1990s, a small group of women remained at the camp until 2000 as an ongoing symbol of resistance to nuclear weapons.

## Women Peacekeepers

In January 2007, the first all-women peacekeeping unit of the United Nations arrived in Liberia. Made up of about one hundred Indian policewomen, the unit was sent to the capital, Monrovia, to work alongside the other 15,000-strong peacekeeping force already in the country. This unique women-only group hoped to appear more approachable to women and children. They are working as police officers who train local police and can also act as a rapid reaction force for crowd control. Their installation was a response to the problems of 2006, when relief organizations accused male UN peacekeepers in Liberia of trading food for sex with girls made homeless from the war.[6] The Liberian peacekeepers are only there thanks to a landmark breakthrough in peacekeeping for women, UN Security Council Resolution 1325, passed on October 30, 2000, which stressed the importance of involving women in all aspects of peacekeeping operations.[7]

Rachel Mayanja, UN Special Adviser on Gender Issues and the Advancement of Women, said the adoption of Resolution 1325 had "fundamentally changed the image of women, from that of being exclusively victims of war to that of active participants, as peacemakers, peacebuilders and negotiators."[8]

## A Level Playing Field

*It's very, very important in a Muslim environment to have the father as a leader of the family that believes in you and lets you continue to do what you want. And my father played a very major role in my life. He could have said within seconds "I want you to stay home, get married and have kids." But my father understood at the moment where I started to run that my destiny was in sports, but I had to do very well in my education. I also had to do my work in the house, clear up and wash the dishes. This was number one, then my education was number two and then athletics was number three . . .*

*Just before we headed off to Los Angeles for the 1984 Olympics, the King of Morocco called us into the palace to wish us good luck. As he was delivering his speech he said "I'd like you to bring back a gold medal, either a man or a woman." As we were a team composed of about 120 athletes, all men and I was the only female, I understood he was speaking to me. I think it is something that I had to do, and I think with my courage I contributed a little bit to sport and athletics in my country and in the Arab states, and in Africa.*

—Hurdler Nawal El Moutawakel, who won the gold
medal at the Los Angeles Olympics in 1984,
becoming the first woman from an Islamic country
to win a medal and the first Moroccan athlete
of either sex to win a gold medal.[9]

## Unsporting History

Women in ancient Greece were rarely allowed to take part in sports. They were banned from competing in the Olympic games, and married women were even barred from attending the games as spectators, although prostitutes or virgins were allowed. The Greek historian Pausanias tells the story of Callipateira, who broke this rule to see her son compete:

> She being a widow, disguised herself exactly like a gymnastic trainer, and brought her son to compete at Olympia. Peisirodus, for so her son was called, was victorious, and Callipateira, as she was jumping over the enclosure in which they kept the trainers shut up, bared her person. So her sex was discovered, but they let her go unpunished out of respect for her father, her brothers and her son, all of whom had been victorious at Olympia. But a law was passed that in future, trainers should strip before entering the arena.[10]

Winners of the men's chariot races were often given women as their prize. Athletic women weren't given their own games in the Olympic Stadium until the sixth century B.C., called the Heraea Games and, surprisingly enough, they didn't get men as prizes, but pomegranates—symbols of fertility.

At the first modern Olympic Games in 1896, women were not allowed to compete. It wasn't until 1900 that woman did take part, when the games were staged in Paris simultaneously with the World's Fair Exhibition. Women took part in tennis, golf, ballooning, croquet, equestrianism, and yachting events in 1900, and Charlotte Cooper became the first woman to win an Olympic medal, for singles tennis. Track and field athletics proved the biggest hurdle for women—they weren't allowed to compete in that event until the 1928 Olympic games in Amsterdam. For nearly a century, from 1896 to1981, all the members of the International Olympic Committee were men.

## Why Don't Women Play Sports?

Cultural stereotypes, religious considerations, embarrassment, and lack of encouragement all contribute to women's low participation in competitive sports to differing degrees all over the world. Constraints and fears about girls being outside in a public place prevent them from taking part in informal games of street football or cricket, which boys all over the world play. Expectations of girl children to help with housework and domestic chores also cut into their leisure time, unlike that of their brothers.

Negative ideas of sports being "unfeminine" often prevail—that it is somehow wrong for women and girls to be aggressive and competitive, to get sweaty, and to be physically active in public. The under-representation of women's sports in the media also devalues their importance, and this lack of both visibility and role models for girls have the side effect of making girls reluctant to take up sports. In 2006 in the British press, only 5.2 percent of all sports journalism was devoted to female sports. Out of the 610 members of the Sports Journalist Association of Great Britain, only around 10 percent are women.[11]

> She shouldn't be here. I know that sounds sexist but I am sexist. This is not park football, so what are women doing here? . . . It is bad enough with the incapable referees and linesmen we have but if you start bringing in women, you have big problems.[12]

This is what the manager of the Luton soccer team, Mike Newell, said in 2006 after referee Amy Rayner failed to award a penalty to his side at a crucial moment in a game.

## Spectator Sport

Women are often relegated to the sidelines in sports, cheering on their husbands and sons, facilitating their success by playing a supporting role. There is a demographic force in U.S. politics called the "soccer mom": a mother who ferries her child to soccer practice four times or more a week. In the 2008 U.S. presidential election campaign, Sarah Palin, the Republican vice presidential nominee, described herself as a "hockey mom" and attempted to make political virtue of this. In the United Kingdom, wives and girlfriends traditionally take turns washing the teams' uniforms for their male partners and children, and they are usually given, or take on, the job of providing food after the match.

In Iran, after the revolution of 1979, women were banned from even being spectators at sporting events. For twenty-seven years they haven't been able to watch the national soccer team play; the reason given is that it exposes women to rough language in close proximity to male strangers. In April 2006 President Mahmoud Ahmadinejad briefly lifted the ban after combined pressure from Iranian woman activists and the impact of a film called *Offside,* the subject of which was women soccer fans disguising themselves as men in order to go to the Azadi Stadium in Tehran.

In a scene from the film, one of the girls talks to the young army conscript who is guarding them after they've been discovered and are being held in a room:

> "Why were Japanese women allowed into the stadium for the World Cup qualifying match in 2005?"
> "Because they're Japanese."
> "So my problem is I was born in Iran."

President Ahmadinejad's stated reasoning for letting women in was aimed at placating Islamic hardliners. "The presence of women and families in public places promotes chastity," he said. However, it was such a controversial decision that religious leaders stepped in and decided that it was "un-Islamic for a woman to look at a strange man's legs—even if she didn't take pleasure from it." Two months later the president was forced to back down. Iran's female soccer fans are once again unable to watch their national team. However, playing soccer is increasingly popular among Iranian women, and there is a national Iranian women's soccer team that competes internationally, although they have separate facilities and are barred from training or playing in the same national stadiums as men.

## More Prizes for Some

It has taken thirty-nine years for women tennis players at Wimbledon to receive the same prize money as men.

The decision was made for the 2007 tournament, under pressure from tennis stars like Venus Williams, John McEnroe, and Maria Sharapova. The year before, the women's prize was 95 percent of the men's, so the difference in prize money was more a symbolic statement than an economic decision, indicating that women's competitive tennis was considered to be of lesser value than men's. In 2007, Billie Jean King, six-time Wimbledon singles champion and pioneer for equality in the game, discounted the old argument that men get paid more because they play the best of five sets while women play the best of three:

> Entertainers don't get paid by the hour. They just get paid, period. It's a done deal.[13]

The success of many pioneering women in sports has inspired others to follow; Tanni Grey-Thompson is one of these pioneers. Born with spina bifida, Grey-Thompson lost the use of her legs when she was five. She now holds thirteen Paralympic medals for wheelchair racing, nine of them gold:

> I grew up in a sporty family which made it easy for me. I was one of those kids at school who tried every sport. I had a go at everything. I tried swimming, archery, basketball and tennis. Eventually I found athletics, and I've never looked back.[14]

*Eighty year old Ratna Maya Thapa from the central region of Nepal shows her voter registration card after walking for one and a half hours to cast her ballot in the Nepalese Constituent Assembly elections. UN photo/Nayan Tara.*

## Justice for All

*Everyone has the right to take part in the government of their country, directly or through freely chosen representatives.*

—Article 21 of the Universal Declaration
of Human Rights 1948

*DAILY SKETCH,* Thursday June 5, 1913
HISTORY'S MOST WONDERFUL DERBY:
FIRST HORSE DISQUALIFIED
A 100 to 1 Chance Wins
Suffragette Nearly Killed by the King's Colt

That was the order of importance the *Daily Sketch* accorded to the top news stories coming out of the Epsom Derby in 1913. One of the most militant of suffragettes, Emily Davison, had already thrown rocks at Prime Minister David Lloyd-George, burned down mailboxes, and, when in Strangeways Prison, nearly died after refusing force-feeding. On June 4, she ran onto the racecourse and tried to grab the bridle of the racehorse Anmer, owned by King George V. She was knocked unconscious and never recovered.

Five years later, women in Britain who were over thirty, householders or married to householders, occupied property with an annual rent of five pounds, or were university graduates were allowed to vote. It was another ten years before all women had voting rights equal to those of men.

But Britain wasn't a trailblazer. In 1893 New Zealand was the first state to grant universal suffrage for women, followed by Australia, the Scandinavian countries, the then USSR, Germany, Canada, and Poland. In the century that followed, legal reform brought universal suffrage to the vast majority of countries. At the beginning of the twenty-first century, only Saudi Arabia still denies women the right to vote. Other countries have partial or limited suffrage, like Lebanon, which has compulsory suffrage for men who are over twenty-one; women can vote if they want to, but they are required to have proof of elementary education. Bhutan allows one vote per house, available to men or women, which in practice means more men than women vote. Since 1962 the kingdom of Brunei has no suffrage for either men or women.

## Women and the Law

> *Civil laws that appear to have little to do with violence also have an impact on women's ability to protect themselves and assert their rights. Laws that restrict women's right to divorce or inheritance, or that prevent them from gaining custody of their children, receiving financial compensation or owning property, all serve to make women dependent on men and limit their ability to leave a violent situation.*[15]
>
> —United Nations Development Fund
> for Women (UNIFEM)

Male primogeniture, which means that the eldest son inherits his father's estate, has been the prevailing method of passing property and wealth for generations in Britain. Primogeniture ensures the perpetuation of a ruling elite class, and also keeps women reliant on their fathers, husbands, or brothers for financial security. Up until the late 1800s in Britain, the law regarded a married couple as one person; the husband was responsible for his wife, and any personal property she brought to the marriage automatically became his. In 1870 the Married Women's Property Act in Britain finally allowed women to keep their earnings and inherit personal property and money. However, the golden age for equality of inheritance in Britain appears to have been in Anglo-Saxon England; in the seventh century, King Aethelbert's law number 79 said about divorce: "If she wish to go away with her children, let her have half the property." This gave a woman security and independence, but such enlightened laws were lost with the Norman Conquest in 1066.[16]

Asma Khada, a lawyer and human rights activist, says that "family law is the key to the gate of freedom and human rights for women." In Sharia, or Islamic law, a woman keeps the money and property she owns after marriage. This was an extremely progressive concept when it was instituted 1,400 years ago, and it still is today in many parts of the world. Also, a woman's consent has to be obtained for marriage. If a marriage is proved to be forced, without the consent of either party, it is not acceptable under Islam and can be annulled by a Sharia Council. The varying degrees to which Islamic law is enforced in Muslim countries is based on specific interpretation of the Koran and the Hadith (the oral tradition related to the sayings and conduct of the prophet Mohammed), and men have traditionally held the power of interpretation. As with any culture or religion, Islam isn't static; and women's groups are active in carving out their own space and rights within the religion, particularly with regard to family law.

Aina Khan is a Muslim woman who is a lawyer living in London. Her family comes from Pakistan, and she specializes in a tricky but growing area of law: the recognition of Sharia family law by English courts when problems arise. She says one common problem is that Muslim women don't get their marriages registered at a civil ceremony when they marry in the United Kingdom, not realizing that registration is essential for them to have recognized rights as a wife rather than just a cohabitee. At the time of a Muslim marriage, a sum of money known as the Haq Mehr is handed over by the husband to his wife; it is intended to give her enough to live on after divorce or widowhood. This amount is written down in the marriage contract, or Nikah Nameh. Khan says that when a husband refuses to pay the Haq Mehr, she is able to use English law to enforce his obligation. She says:

> Also, the use of prenuptial agreements is becoming more common in the UK. The "Nikah Nameh," or Islamic marriage certificate, can be viewed as such an agreement, since it addresses the issue of the financial settlement and is signed before witnesses.[17]

But as with any discussion of Islamic law, customs vary throughout the world. In Iran the contract includes many provisions including the right of divorce that can be transferred to women.

## Progressive Laws

In 1956 a postcolonial, newly independent Tunisia reformed family law. The government outlawed polygamy and abolished repudiation, which is the unilateral right in Islam of a man to end his marriage without going to court. Divorce could now only take place in a Tunisian court, and women were allowed to file for divorce on the same grounds as men. It increased a mother's custody rights and expanded inheritance rights for daughters and grand-daughters. The Tunisian reforms became a yardstick for other Middle Eastern countries regarding family law. The Convention on the Elimination of All Forms of Discrimination against Women (CEDAW) recognized this in 1995:

> " One of Tunisia's greatest achievements since in-dependence is the body of laws which [gave] women rights not enjoyed anywhere else in the Arab world.

## What Happens When Women Are the Lawmakers?

Lawmaking, refining, and judging have all been almost ex-clusively male preserves from the Roman laws of Justin-ian until very recently. But what happens when women are the lawmakers?

In Rwanda, after the terrible 1994 genocide, women were crucial in rebuilding the country again. In the par-liamentary elections of 2008, 56 percent of the seats were won by women, making Rwanda the first country in the world where women outnumber men in parliament. In 1999 the Rwanda Inheritance Law was passed, giving wid-ows the right to inherit their husband's property and also granting equal rights of inheritance to male and female children. As traditional law in Rwanda denies women in-heritance rights, human rights activists are waging a na-tionwide educational campaign to bring the news of the legal changes to the whole of Rwandan society. Other leg-islation on marriage, child rape, and violence against women has been amended to protect women's rights, but again customary law, which often overrides written law through ignorance of the civil code and lack of access to legal advice, remains biased against women. Only through addressing the imbalance of girls' access to education and political empowerment in Rwanda will lasting change, and a fully equal society, be brought about.[18]

## Sometimes Laws Aren't Enough

In India, laws were passed in 1956 to protect women's right to inherit property from their fathers, but despite this law, such inheritance often doesn't happen because women themselves remain ignorant of these rights. Change is happening slowly, helped by the "due diligence" clause of the 1979 Convention on the Elimination of All Forms of Discrimination against Women. This means that individual states have a duty of care to make sure that individual citizens know their legal rights and have access to lawyers to implement them; countries that have ratified the Convention are legally bound to put its provisions into practice. They have to submit national reports, at least every four years, on measures they have taken to comply with their treaty obligations.

## A Breakthrough for Women's Rights

The Rome Statute of the International Criminal Court came into force in 2002; it specifically defines rape and other gender-based violence during conflict as "war crimes, crimes against humanity and components of the crime of genocide as well as torture." This is a dramatic step forward in thinking to take rape out of the private, domestic sphere; instead it defines the perpetrator as an agent of the state, an armed political group, or a religious extremist organization. This law came out of intense women's activism: women's groups and nongovernmental organizations played a fundamental role in all preparatory meetings to ensure that abuses against women got into statute books. The statute also makes practical suggestions, including the need to hire judges and prosecutors with special expertise in crimes against humanity and war crimes for these cases. The court's first judges were elected in February 2003; among the eighteen judges, seven are women, a historic achievement. The Rome Statute came out of the work done in the International Tribunals for the former Yugoslavia and for Rwanda—out of so much human misery there came at least some progress for women's legal rights.

The history of women's rights, and the legal changes that have marked improvements for women's lives all over the world, are undeniably positive achievements in the last hundred years or more. However, the marker of real improvement for women must be to create better opportunities, less discrimination, and a more equal society for each new generation of daughters that come along.

Controversial, powerful women who occupy the world stage often face opprobrium and censure in equal parts with admiration and envy from the rest of society—both men and women. However, they also often change our opinions of the potential and possibilities out there for all women, and subtly alter the space women occupy in the world. The last word goes to two of these women:

> " I'm tough, I'm ambitious, and I know exactly what I want. If that makes me a bitch, okay.
> —Madonna Ciccone

> " Whether women are better than men I cannot say—but I can say they are certainly no worse.
> —Golda Meir

# Notes

Amnesty International publishes numerous reports on human rights violations around the world. Reports cited below are listed by their index number; they can be accessed at http://www.amnesty.org/en/library and downloaded free of charge.

## Introduction

1. Kofi Annan, secretary general of the United Nations from 1997 to 2007, speaking in 1999.
2. The UN Founding Charter of 1945, www.un.org/aboutun/charter.
3. UN Convention on the Elimination of All Forms of Discrimination against Women (CEDAW), 1979, www.un.org/womenwatch/daw/cedaw/.
4. Amnesty International, "Respect, Protect and Fulfil Women's Human Rights: State Responsibility for Abuses by 'Non-state Actors,'" August 31, 2000, AI index number 10R 50/001/200.
5. *The Times* (London), April 13, 2007.
6. *My Century,* BBC World Service, 1999.

## Chapter 1

1. Jean-Jacques Rousseau, *Émile ou de l'éducation,* book 5. Originally published in 1762.
2. Mary Wollstonecraft, *A Vindication of the Rights of Women.* Originally published in 1792. (Harmondsworth, U.K.: Penguin, 2004), 105–106.
3. "Labour-Saving Hints and Ideas for the Home" (George Routledge & Sons Ltd., 1924; repr. 1992).
4. Charlotte Gill, *Daily Mail,* October 26, 2006. Article based on a survey commissioned by Vitabiotics Wellwoman, a vitamin supplement

for women, http://www.dailymail.co.uk/pages/live/articles/news/news.html?in_article_id=412178&in_page_id=1770.

5. Report by the Equal Opportunities Commission, May 2007, www.cehr.org.uk/. This was the last report before the EOC was absorbed into the Commission for Equality and Human Rights.

6. *My Century,* BBC World Service, 1999.

7. See www.niputesnisoumises.com.

8. Patricia Smith Butcher, *Education for Equality: Women's Rights Periodicals and Women's Higher Education, 1849–1920* (New York, London: Greenwood Press, 1990).

9. Mary Wollstonecraft, *A Vindication of the Rights of Women* (Harmondsworth, U.K.: Penguin, 2004).

10. Joint report by UNAIDS/UNFPA/UNIFEM, "Women and HIV/AIDS: Confronting the Crisis," July 2004, http://www.unfpa.org/hiv/women/report/index.htm.

11. Glyn Strong, "Courage under Fire," *Telegraph Magazine,* 2007.

12. *Global Framework,* Beijing Conference on Women 1995.

13. Amnesty International, "Women, HIV/AIDS and Human Rights," November 4, 2004, AI index number ACT 77/084/2004.

14. Michael Noer, "Don't Marry Career Women," *Forbes,* August 2006, http://www.forbes.com/2006/08/23/Marriage-Careers-Divorce_cx_mn_land.html.

15. Barry Wigmore, "Just Why Are Women Unhappier Than Men?" *Daily Mail,* September 17, 2007, http://www.dailymail.co.uk/pages/live/articles/news/news.html?in_article_id=484134&in_page_id=17.

16. Amnesty International, "Israel: Conflict, Occupation and Patriarchy: Women Carry the Burden," March 31, 2005, AI index number MDE 15/016/2005.

17. Amnesty International, "Killings in Guatemala Continue Unchallenged," November 2005, AI index number AMR 34/043/2005. See also "Guatemala: No Protection, No Justice: Killings of Women in Guatemala," June 8, 2005, AI index number AMR 34/017/2005.

18. Amnesty International, "Claudina Velasquez—Guatemala," http://www.amnesty.org.uk/content.asp?CategoryID=11407.

19. Anna Politkovskaya, *A Russian Diary,* trans. Arch Tait (Harvill Secker, 2007).

20. Jim Ballard, interview with *The Observer,* March 30, 2003.

21. Quoted in Nadia Al-Sakkaf, "Testimonies over Time: When Women Are Violated for Saying 'Here We Are,'" *Yemen Times,* April 2007, http://www.yementimes.com/article.shtml?i=1039&p=report&a=1.

22. Ibid.

23. All four quotations from "Swept under the Rug: Abuses against Domestic Workers around the World," *Human Rights Watch* 18, no. 7 (July 2006).

24. World Bank, "HIV/AIDS in Sri Lanka," August 2008, http://site resources.worldbank.org/INTSAREGTOPHIVAIDS/Resources/496350–1217345766462/HIV-AIDS-brief-Aug08-LK.pdf.

25. Amnesty International, "Gulf Cooperation Council (GCC) Countries: Women Deserve Dignity and Respect," May 11, 2005, AI index number MDE04/004/2005.

26. Mende Nazer and Damien Lewis, *Slave* (London: Virago Press, 2004).

27. "Swept under the Rug: Abuses against Domestic Workers around the World," *Human Rights Watch* 18, no. 7 (July 2006).

28. End Child Prostitution, Child Pornography and the Trafficking of Children for Sexual Purposes (ECPAT), "New Report Shows Significant Gaps in Government Policy on Trafficked Children in UK," September 20, 2007, http://www.ecpat.org.uk/press_03.html.

29. International Labour Organisation (ILO) Report for International Women's Day 2006, "More, but Not Always Better Jobs for Women in Latin America," February 28, 2006, http://www.ilo.org/global/Themes/Working_Conditions/Wages/lang—en/WCMS_067504/index.htm.

30. *My Century,* BBC World Service, 1999.

31. "The Gender Agenda—The Unfinished Revolution," July 2007, www.equalityhumanrights.com/Documents/Gender/General%20advice%20and%20information/EOC%20Gender%20agenda.pdf.

32. Research by Linda Babcock, professor of economics at Carnegie Mellon University, published in *The Guardian,* August 21, 2007, http://www.guardian.co.uk/world/2007/aug/21/gender.pay.

33. Shankar Vedantam, "The Truth about Why Women Are Paid Less—Even If They Ask for More," *The Guardian,* August 21, 2007. Information on the Harvard study available at http://www.hks.harvard.edu/news-events/news/articles/bowles.

34. Ibid.

35. Carolyn Hannan, "A New World: A Vision for Gender Equality and Empowerment of Women" (address, United Nations Department of Economic and Social Affairs to the Contemporary Women Program, Brescia University, April 6, 2006).

36. CEO Forum Group, "Retaining Talented Women," Spring 2007, www.ceoforum.com.au/article-detail.cfm?cid=6364.

37. Catalyst, nonprofit women's research institute in New York, www.catalyst.org.

38.   *Women at the Top,* BBC World Service, 1994.

39.   Rachel Sylvester and Alice Thomson, "Immigration Is Not the Problem," *The Daily Telegraph,* September 29, 2007, http://www.telegraph.co.uk/news/uknews/1564557/Immigration-is-not-the-problem.html.

40.   Jacqui Goddard, "Pamela Melroy: A Giant Leap for Womankind," *The Times* (London), October 23, 2007, http://women.times online.co.uk/tol/life_and_style/women/the_way_we_live/article 2718202.ece.

41.   *My Century,* BBC World Service, 1999.

42.   Current statistics on the number of women in national parliaments can be found on the website of the Inter-Parliamentary Union, www.ipu.org/wmn-e/world.

43.   "Women Break into African Politics," *Africa Recovery* 18, no. 1 (April 2004), 4, http://www.un.org/ecosocdev/geninfo/afrec/vol18 no1/181women.htm.

44.   Current statistics for Rwandan women politicians can be found at www.ipu.org/wmn-e/classif.

45.   Glyn Strong, "Malalai Joya: Courage under Fire," *Telegraph Magazine,* September 29, 2007, http://www.telegraph.co.uk/arts/main .jhtml?xml=/arts/2007/09/29/sm_joya.xml.

## Chapter 2

1.   Benazir Bhutto, interview for *Women In Power,* BBC World Service, 1992.

2.   William Shakespeare, *The Taming of the Shrew,* act 5, scene 2, lines 146–153.

3.   *People's Daily Online,* "China Has 37 Million More Males than Females," July 6, 2007, http://english.peopledaily.com.cn/90001/ 90776/90882/6212115.html.

4.   Therese Hesketh, Li Lu, and Zhu Wei Xing, "The Effect of China's One-Child Family Policy after 25 Years," *The New England Journal of Medicine* 353, no. 11 (September 15, 2005): 1171–1176.

5.   Catherine Deveney, "The High Price of Freedom," *The Scotsman,* February 4, 2007, http://news.scotsman.com/topics.cfm?tid=612 &id=171442007.

6.   Amnesty International, "France: Violence against Women: A Matter for the State," February 8, 2006, AI index number EUR21/001/2006; comments reported in Marie-Hélène Franjou, "Prévention de la pratique des mariages forcés, Délégation régionale aux droits des femmes," Commission pour l'abolition des mutila-

tions sexuelles (Committee for the Abolition of Genital Mutilation), Regional Delegation for Women's Rights, 2000.

7. United Kingdom, Home Office Report, "Dealing with Cases of Forced Marriage," 1st ed., November 2005, http://publications .teachernet.gov.uk/eOrderingDownload/FCO%2075263.pdf.

8. "The Law Made Simple," (The Chaucer Press, 1981). See also: http://www.hiddenhurt.co.uk/Articles/maritalrape.htm.

9. Equality Now, "Words and Deeds: Holding Governments Accountable in the Beijing+10 Review Process," http://www.equality now.org/english/wan/beijing10/laws_en.html.

10. "La violence au sein des couples, les femmes brisent le silence : améliorons la loi," symposium, March 31, 2005. Taken from Amnesty International, "France: Violence against Women: A Matter for the State," February 6, 2006, AI index number EUR21/ 001/2006.

11. Amnesty International, "France: Violence against Women: A Matter for the State," February 6, 2006, AI index number EUR21/ 001/2006.

12. Catherine MacKinnon, interview by Stuart Jeffries, *The Guardian*, April 12, 2006.

13. Amnesty International, "Sexual Violence against Women and Girls in Jamaica: 'Just a Little Sex,'" June 22, 2006, AI index number AMR 38/002/2006.

14. For more information on women, immigration status, and domestic violence see WomensAid website, http://www.womensaid.org .uk/domestic_violence_topic.asp?section=0001000100220041&sec tionTitle=Domestic+violence+%28general%29.

15. Amnesty International, "The Russian Federation: Nowhere to Turn to: Violence against Women in the Family," December 14, 2005, AI index number EUR 46/056/2005.

16. Russian Federation, *Fifth Periodic Report of State Parties to the Committee on the Elimination of Discrimination against Women*, March 3, 1999, CEDAW/C/USR/5.

17. Amnesty International, "The Russian Federation: Nowhere to Turn to: Violence against Women in the Family," December 14, 2005, AI index number EUR 46/056/2005.

18. "Ending the Cycle of Domestic Violence," *The Guardian*, July 24, 2006.

19. "All the time my husband was beating me, he was telling me this was the day I was going to die," *The Observer*, May 13, 2007.

20. Lynn Welchman and Sara Hossain, *"Honour": Crimes, Paradigms and Violence against Women* (London and New York: Zed Books, 2006).

21. For more information about Madadgaar, see http://www.madadgaar .org/.

22. "A Bad Ancient Tradition," *The Economist,* April 12, 2007, http:// www.economist.com/world/europe/displaystory.cfm?story_id=9009 023.

23. Nathaniel Hawthorne, *The Scarlet Letter,* first published 1850.

24. Tess Stimson, "Want to Save Your Marriage? Ignore Your Children!" *Daily Mail,* October 26, 2006, http://www.dailymail.co.uk/pages/ live/femail/article.html?in_article_id=412669&in_page_id=1879.

25. "Law Punishes Victims of Rape in Pakistan," *The Wire,* July 2004, http://web.amnesty.org/wire/July2004/Pakistan.

26. Amnesty International, "Iran: Amnesty International outraged at reported execution of a 16 year old girl," August 22, 2004, AI index number MDE 13/036/2004.

27. "The Execution of a Teenage Girl," BBC broadcast, July 27, 2004.

28. Amnesty International, "Iran: Amnesty International outraged at reported execution of a 16 year old girl," August 22, 2004, AI index number MDE 13/036/2004.

29. Syed Shoaib Hasan, "Strong Feelings over Pakistan's Rape Laws," BBC news online, November 15, 2006, http://news.bbc.co.uk/1/hi/ world/south_asia/6152520.stm.

30. Saint Augustine of Hippo, "De bono conjugali" ("On the Good of Marriage"), c. 410.

31. Hannah Koroma, Women's Officer for Amnesty International in Sierra Leone, "Female Genital Mutilation, a Human Rights Issue," October 1, 1997, AI index number ACT 77/12/97.

32. UNICEF Report, "Domestic Violence against Women and Children," 2000.

33. Hannah Koroma, Women's Officer for Amnesty International in Sierra Leone, "Female Genital Mutilation, a Human Rights Issue," October 1, 1997, AI index number ACT 77/12/97.

34. World Health Organization, "Progress in Sexual and Reproductive Health," no. 72, 2006, http://www.who.int/reproductivehealth/hrp/ progress/72.pdf.

35. Joint statement by the World Health Organization, the UN Children's Fund (UNICEF), and the UN Population Fund, February 1996.

36. UNICEF Report, Women of Senegal—Tostan movement, "Domestic Violence Against Women and Children" 2000, 15.

37. World Health Organization, "Progress in Sexual and Reproductive Health," no. 72, 2006, http://www.who.int/reproductive-health/ hrp/progress/72.pdf.

38. Sandy Kobrin, "More Women Seek Vaginal Plastic Surgery," *Women's Enews,* November 14, 2004, http://www.womensenews .org/article.cfm/dyn/aid/2067/context/archive.

39. "Achieving Equality Is about More Than Just Changing the Law," *Ghanaian Chronicle,* April 4, 2007.

40. "India Wife Dies on Husband's Pyre," BBC News Online, August 22, 2006, http://news.bbc.co.uk/1/hi/world/south_asia/5273336 .stm.

41. Lucy Ash, "India's Dowry Deaths," BBC Radio 4's Crossing Continents, July 16, 2003, http://news.bbc.co.uk/1/hi/programmes/ crossing_continents/3071963.stm.

42. In a study by Women in Law in 2005, one third of countries in southern Africa were said to practice widow cleansing. Sharon LaFraniere, "AIDS Now Compels Africa to Challenge Widows' 'Cleansing,'" *The New York Times,* May 11, 2005, http://www.ny times.com/2005/05/11/international/africa/11malawi.html.

43. Human Rights Watch, "Fact Sheet: HIV/AIDS and Women's Property Rights in Africa," www.hrw.org/campaigns/women/property/ aidsfactsheet.htm.

44. To read the Women and Young Offenders handbook in full, see http://www.hmprisonservice.gov.uk/assets/documents/1000028710 000160pib_female.pdf.

45. Amnesty International USA, *Women in Prison: A Fact Sheet,* http:// www.amnestyusa.org/women/womeninprison.html.

46. Ibid.

47. Ruth Chigwada-Bailey, "Black Women's Experiences of the Criminal Justice System," www.black-history-month.co.uk/articles/black womensexperiences.html.

48. Amnesty International USA, "Stop Violence Against Women," *Women in Prison: A Fact Sheet,* http://www.amnestyusa.org/women/ womeninprison.html.

49. Amnesty International, "USA: 'Not Part of My Sentence': Violations of the Human Rights of Women in Custody," March 1, 1999, AI index number AMR 51/019/1999.

50. Justice for Women, www.jfw.org.uk, and Southall Black Sisters www.southallblacksisters.org.uk/campaigns.html.

## Chapter 3

1. Jung Chang and John Halliday, *Mao: The Unknown Story* (Jonathan Cape, 2005), 154.

2. *My Century,* BBC World Service, 1999.
3. Maureen Dellanian, *My Century,* BBC World Service, 1999.
4. Amnesty International, "Women, HIV/AIDS and Human Rights," November 4, 2004, AI index number ACT 77/084/2004.
5. Amnesty International, "Kenya: Rape: The Invisible Crime," March 8, 2002, AI index number AFR 32/001/2002.
6. Kate Burt, "Whatever Happened to the Femidom?" *The Guardian,* August 23, 2005. See also www.the-pleasure-project.org.
7. Suggested slogans for pro-life marchers from cul.detmich.com/slogans.html.
8. "Abortions 'crisis' Threatens NHS," BBC News, April 16, 2007, http://news.bbc.co.uk/1/hi/health/6558823.stm.
9. Jeremy Laurance, "Abortion Crisis As Doctors Refuse to Perform Surgery," *The Independent,* April 16, 2007.
10. Jack Hitt, "Pro-Life Nation," *The New York Times,* April 9, 2006, http://www.nytimes.com/2006/04/09/magazine/09abortion.html.

## Chapter 4

1. Lisa Takeuchi Cullen, "Changing Faces," *Time,* 2006, http://www.time.com/time/asia/covers/1101020805/story.html.
2. Dan McDougall, "Trade in Hair Forces India's Children to Pay the Price," *The Observer,* June 25, 2006, http://observer.guardian.co.uk/world/story/0,1805328,00.html.
3. Ian Cobain and Adam Luck, "The Beauty Products from the Skin of Executed Chinese Prisoners," *The Guardian,* September 13, 2005, http://www.guardian.co.uk/china/story/0,7369,1568622,00.html.
4. Amnesty International, "Japan: Still Waiting after 60 Years: Justice for Survivors of Japan's Military Sexual Slavery System," October 27, 2005, AI index number ASA 22/012/2005.
5. Ibid.
6. *The Geneva Convention Relative to the Treatment of Prisoners of War,* 1949, which came into force the following year, http://www.unhchr.ch/html/menu3/b/91.htm#top.
7. Amnesty International, The International Criminal Court, Fact Sheet 7, "Ensuring Justice for Women," April 12, 2005, AI index number IOR 40/006/2005.
8. Amnesty International, "Rwanda 'Marked for Death': Rape Survivors Living with HIV/AIDS in Rwanda," April 5, 2004, AI index number 47/007/2004.

9. All statistics and their sources come from Amnesty International press release, "Making Violence against Women Count: Facts and Figures—a Summary," March 5, 2004, http://news.amnesty.org/index/ENGACT770342004.

10. T. S. Nelson, *For Love of Country: Confronting Rape and Sexual Harassment in the U.S. Military* (Binghamton and London: Haworth Maltreatment and Trauma Press, 2002).

11. Professor Helen Benedict, Columbia School of Journalism, from her interview with Democracy Now! "The Private War of Women Soldiers: Female Vet, Soldier Speak Out on Rising Sexual Assault within US Military," March 8, 2007, http://www.democracynow.org/article.pl?sid=07/03/08/1443232.

12. Marjorie Cohn, "Military Hides Cause of Women Soldier's Deaths," January 30, 2006, http://www.truthout.org/article/military-hides-cause-women-soldiers-deaths.

13. Professor Helen Benedict, Columbia School of Journalism, from her interview with Democracy Now! "The Private War of Women Soldiers: Female Vet, Soldier Speak Out on Rising Sexual Assault within US Military," March 8, 2007, http://www.democracynow.org/article.pl?sid=07/03/08/1443232.

14. Survey by Equal Opportunities Commission and British Ministry of Defence, http://83.137.212.42/sitearchive/eoc/PDF/S-R%20Report_Executive_Summary.pdf?page=18798. General information on sexual harassment and the British armed forces available on the Equal Opportunities website, http://www.equalityhumanrights.com/en/newsandcomment/Pages/Investigationintosexualharassmentinthearmedforcesends.aspx.

15. Interview with author, Manila, the Philippines, 1996.

16. Joan Smith, "Why British Men Are Rapists," *New Statesman,* January 2006, http://www.newstatesman.com/200601230006.

17. The Poppy Project newsletter, January 2006, www.eaves4women.co.uk/POPPY_Project/POPPY_Project.php.

18. Ibid.

19. "The Total Film Interview—Quentin Tarantino," *Total Film,* November 21, 2007, http://www.totalfilm.com/features/the-total-film-interview-quentin-tarantino.

20. Internet Watch Foundation Annual report, April 17, 2007, http://www.iwf.org.uk/documents/20080417_iwf_annual_report_2007_(web).pdf.

21. Kira Cochrane, "For Your Entertainment," *The Guardian,* May 1, 2007. http://www.guardian.co.uk/film/2007/may/01/gender.world.

22. Interview with author, February 2005.

## Chapter 5

1. Richard H. Robbins, *Global Problems and the Culture of Capitalism* (Boston: Allyn and Bacon, 1999), 354.
2. Amartya Sen, "Population and Gender Equity," *The Nation*, July 24/31, 2000.
3. Susan Buckingham-Hatfield, *Gender and Environment* (London: Routledge, 2000).
4. United Nations Population Fund, "The State of the World Population Report 2001," chapter 4, http://www.unfpa.org/swp/2001/english/ch04.html.
5. Shahidur R. Khandker and Christopher Udry, "Gender, Property Rights, and Resource Management in Ghana," World Bank Research Program 1997, abstract available at http://www.worldbank.org/html/dec/Publications/Abstracts97/03esd/esd18.html.
6. Banda Aceh, "The Tsunami's Impact on Women," Oxfam, 2005, http://www.oxfam.org.uk/what_we_do/issues/conflict_disasters/bn_tsunami_women.htm.
7. "Profile: Wangari Maathai," BBC News Online, October 8, 2004, http://news.bbc.co.uk/1/hi/world/africa/3726084.stm.
8. Radhika Coomaraswamy, "Preliminary Report Submitted by the Special Rapporteur on Violence against Women: Its Causes and Consequences," http://www2.ohchr.org/english/issues/women/rapporteur/. (In April 2006, Radhika Coomaraswamy was appointed as UN Under Secretary General, Special Representative for Children and Armed Conflict.)
9. "Gender and International Society Law and Policy," in *New Millennium New Perspectives: The United Nations, Security and Governance*, ed. R. Thakur and E. Newman, *UN Chronicle* 69, no. 2 (2000): 69–70.
10. Edward Luce, "Gandhi's So Retrograde," *Times* (London), August 18, 2006, http://www.timesonline.co.uk/tol/life_and_style/article611864.ece.
11. War on Want, "Sweatshops and Plantations, Union of Bangladeshi Garment Workers," http://www.waronwant.org/Union%20of%20Bangladeshi%20Garment%20Workers%201722.twl.
12. UNHCR, "Women: Seeking a Better Deal," special issue of *Refugees* Magazine, no. 126, April 2002.
13. Ibid.
14. Ibid.
15. There is a useful website run by the Center for Gender and Refugee Studies that compares laws on gender-based asylum seekers around

the world, and includes the UK Home Office guidelines in full under the UK section, http://cgrs.uchastings.edu/law/gender _guidelines.php#UK.

16. Amnesty International UK, *Down and Out in London: The Road to Destitution for Rejected Asylum Seekers* (London: Amnesty International UK, 2006), www.amnesty.org.uk/content.asp?CategoryID =10682&ArticleID=2727.

17. Women's Commission for Refugee Women and Children, "From The Ground Up, Education and Livelihoods in Southern Sudan," January 2007, http://www.womenscommission.org/pdf/sd_ground .pdf.

## Chapter 6

1. Obituary of Irene Morgan Kirkaldy, *The New York Times,* August 13, 2007.

2. Amr Gharbeia, "Lost In Process," *Index on Censorship* 36, no. 2 (August 2007): 51–55.

3. Dyan Mazurana and Khristopher Carlson, *From Combat to Community: Women and Girls in Sierra Leone,* published by Hunt Alternatives Fund in 2004 as part of its Women Waging Peace program, advocating for the full participation of women in formal and informal peace processes around the world. Available at http://www .smallarmssurvey.org/files/portal/spotlight/disarmament/disarm _pdf/2004_Mazurana_Carlson.pdf.

4. Elisabeth Rehn and Ellen Johnson Sirleaf, *Women, War, Peace: The Independent Experts' Assessment on the Impact of Conflict on Women and Women's Role in Peace-building* (United Nations Development Fund for Women, 2002).

5. Ibid.

6. Jonathan Paye-Layleh, "Women's Unit Arrives in Liberia," *The Guardian,* January 31, 2007, http://www.guardian.co.uk/world/ 2007/jan/31/westafrica.international.

7. United Nations Security Council Resolution 1325 on Women, Peace and Security, http://www.peacewomen.org/un/sc/1325.html.

8. Jane Lloyd, "Women Peacekeepers Making a Difference," *UN Chronicle* 43, no. 1, (2006), http://www.un.org/Pubs/chronicle/ 2006/issue1/0106p06.htm.

9. *My Century,* BBC World Service, 1999.

10. Pausanias, *Description of Greece,* trans. W. H. S. Jones and H. A. Ormerod (Cambridge, MA: Harvard University Press, 1918).

11. The Women's Sports Foundation UK, www.wsf.org.uk.

12.  "Newell Faces Inquiry on 'Sexism,'" BBC Sport, November 12, 2006, http://news.bbc.co.uk/sport1/hi/football/teams/l/luton_town/6140922.stm.

13.  Steve Bierley and Richard Jago, "Wimbledon Ready to Put Women on Same Prize Money as Men," *The Guardian,* February 22, 2007, http://www.guardian.co.uk/sport/2007/feb/22/tennis.gdnsport3.

14.  "Meet Tanni Grey-Thompson," BBC online, November 4, 2005, http://news.bbc.co.uk/sport1/hi/other_sports/disability_sport/4354422.stm.

15.  UNIFEM, "Not a Minute More: Ending Violence against Women," 2003, 104, http://www.unifem.org/filesconfirmed/207/312_book_complete_eng.pdf.

16.  Tanya Saily, "Women in the Middle Ages: Anglo-Saxon England," January 19, 2000, http://www.elisanet.fi/~g632532/aswomen.html.

17.  Aina Khan, "Viewpoint: Women and Sharia Law," BBC News, November 22, 2003, http://news.bbc.co.uk/1/hi/talking_point/special/islam/3198285.stm.

18.  Amnesty International, "Rwanda: 'Marked for Death': Rape Survivors Living with HIV/AIDS in Rwanda," April 6, 2004, AI index number AFR 47/007/2004.

# Sources and Suggestions for Further Information

## Websites

**Amnesty International.** www.amnesty.org.

**ECPAT International** (End Child Prostitution, Child Pornography and the Trafficking of Children for Sexual Purposes). http://www.ecpat.net.

**End Violence Against Women** (EVAW). www.endviolenceagainstwomen.org.uk.

**European Policy Action,** Centre on Violence against Women. www.womenlobby.org.

**Human Rights Watch,** Women's Rights Division. www.hrw.org.

**Internet Watch Foundation,** Internet Porn watchdog. http://www.iwf.org.uk.

**International Centre for Research on Women** (ICRW). www.icrw.org.

**International Labour Organization** (ILO). www.ilo.org.

**Or Does it Explode?** Inside the Struggle for Civil Rights in the Middle East. www.ordoesitexplode.com.

**UNICEF.** www.unicef-icdc.org.

**UN Development Fund for Women** (UNIFEM). www.unifem.org.

**UN Division for the Advancement of Women.** www.un.org/womenwatch/daw.

**UNFPA** (United Nations Population Fund). www.unfpa.org.

**UNHCR.** www.unhcr.org.

**Womankind Worldwide.** www.womankind.org.uk.

**Women's Initiative for Gender Justice.** www.iccwomen.org.

World Health Organization (WHO). http://www.who.int/en/.

## Books and Publications

UN Convention for the Elimination of All Forms of Discrimination against Women (CEDAW). 1979. http://www.un.org/women-watch/daw/cedaw/cedaw.htm.

Bayes, Jane H., and Nayereh Tohidi, eds. *Globalization, Gender, and Religion: The Politics of Women's Rights in Catholic and Muslim Contexts.* Houndmills, Basingstoke, U.K., and New York: Palgrave Macmillan, 2001.

Beauvoir, Simone de. *The Second Sex.* Translated by H. M. Parshley. New York: Alfred A. Knopf, 1993.

Butcher, Patricia Smith. *Education for Equality: Women's Rights Periodicals and Women's Higher Education, 1849–1920.* Contributions in Women's Studies, 111. New York: Greenwood Press, 1989.

Chandra, Sudhir, *Enslaved Daughters, Colonialism, Law and Women's Rights.* 2nd ed. New Delhi and New York: Oxford University Press, 2008.

Charrad, Mounira M. *States and Women's Rights: The Making of Postcolonial Tunisia, Algeria, and Morocco.* Berkeley: University of California Press, 2001.

Coote, Anna, and Tess Gill. *Women's Rights: A Practical Guide.* 3rd ed. Harmondsworth, U.K., and New York: Penguin, 1981.

Crawley, Heaven. *Women as Asylum Seekers: A Legal Handbook.* London: Immigration Law Practitioners' Association, 1997.

Kapoor, Sushma. *Domestic Violence against Women and Girls.* Innocenti Digest 6. Florence, Italy: Innocenti Research Centre, 2000.

Kerr, Joanna, Ellen Sprenger, and Alison Symington, eds. *The Future of Women's Rights: Global Visions and Strategies.* London and New York: ZED Books, 2004.

Kumar, Radha. *The History of Doing: An Illustrated Account of Movements for Women's Rights and Feminism in India, 1800–1990.* London and New York: Verso, 1993.

Levy, Ariel. *Female Chauvinist Pigs: Women and the Rise of Raunch Culture.* New York: Free Press, 2005.

Narain, Vrinda. *Gender and Community: Muslim Women's Rights in India.* Toronto: University of Toronto Press, 2001.

Trouille, Mary Seidman. *Sexual Politics in the Enlightenment: Women Writers Read Rousseau.* Albany: State University of New York Press, 1997.

Wollstonecraft, Mary. *A Vindication of the Rights of Women.* Harmondsworth, U.K.: Penguin, 2004.

Human Rights Watch. "Fact Sheet: HIV/AIDS and Women's Property Rights in Africa." www.hrw.org/campaigns/women/property/aids factsheet.htm.

Universal Declaration of Human Rights. Adopted and proclaimed by General Assembly resolution 217A (III) of 10 December 1948. http://www.un.org/Overview/rights.html.

### Amnesty International Reports

"Broken Bodies, Shattered Minds: Torture and Ill-treatment of Women." March 6, 2001. AI Index: ACT40/001/2001. http://www.amnesty .org/en/library/info/ACT40/001/2001.

"Casualties of War: Women's Bodies, Women's Lives: Stop Crimes against Women in Armed Conflict." October 12, 2004. AI Index: ACT77/ 072/2004. http://www.amnesty.org/en/library/info/ACT77/072/.

"Kosovo (Serbia and Montenegro): 'So does it mean that we have the rights?' Protecting the human rights of women and girls trafficked for forced prostitution in Kosovo." May 6, 2004. AI Index: EU70/ 010/2004. http://www.amnesty.org/en/library/info/EUR70/010/ 2004

"Down and Out in London: The Road to Destitution for Rejected Asylum Seekers." Amnesty International UK, 2006. http://www.amnesty .org.uk/content.asp?CategoryID=10682

"Democratic Republic of Congo: Surviving Rape: Voices from the East." October 25, 2004. AI Index: AFR62/019/2004. http://www.amnesty .org/en/library/info/AFR62/019/2004.

"France: Violence against Women: A Matter for the State." February 6, 2006. AI Index: EUR21/001/2006. http://www.amnesty.org/en/ library/info/EUR21/001/2006.

"What is Female Genital Mutilation?." September 30, 1997. AI Index: ACT 77/006/1997. http://www.amnesty.org/en/library/info/ACT 77/006/1997.

"Gulf Cooperation Council (GCC) Countries: Women Deserve Dignity and Respect." May 10, 2005. AI Index: MDE 04/004/2005. http://www.amnesty.org/en/library/info/MDE%2004/004/2005.

"Japan: Still Waiting after 60 Years: Justice for Survivors of Japan's Military Sexual Slavery System." October 27, 2005. AI Index: ASA 22/012/ 2005. http://www.amnesty.org/en/library/info/ASA22/012/2005/ en.

"Making Rights a Reality: The Duty of States to Address Violence against Women." June 2, 2004. AI Index: ACT 77/049/2004. http://www .amnesty.org/en/library/info/ACT%2077/049/2004.

"Russian Federation: Nowhere to Turn to: Violence against Women in the Family." December 14, 2005. AI Index: EUR 46/056/2005. http://www.amnesty.org/en/library/info/EUR%2046/056/2005.

"Rwanda: 'Marked for Death,' Rape Survivors Living with HIV/AIDS in Rwanda." April 5, 2004. AI Index: AFR 47/007/2004. http://www.amnesty.org/en/library/info/AFR%2047/007/2004.

"Sexual Violence against Women and Girls in Jamaica: 'Just a little sex.'" June 21, 2006. AI Index: AMR 38/002/2006. http://www.amnesty.org/en/library/info/AMR%2038/002/2006.

"Sudan, Darfur: Rape as a Weapon of War: Sexual Violence and Its Consequences." July 19, 2004. AI Index: AFR 54/076/2004. http://www.amnesty.org/en/library/info/AFR%2054/076/2004.

"Women, HIV/AIDS and Human Rights." November 24, 2004. AI Index: ACT 77/084/2004. http://www.amnesty.org/en/library/info/ACT%2077/084/2004.

## Further Information

### On poverty and its disproportionate effect on women:

Economic, Social and Cultural Rights, Effects of Structural Adjustment Programmes on the Full Enjoyment of Human Rights, UN Doc. E/CN.4/1999/50, February 24, 1999.

### On legislation for women's rights enshrined in international treaties:

UN Charter, 1945. http://un.org/aboutun/charter/.

1979 UN Convention on the Elimination of All Forms of Discrimination against Women (CEDAW). http://www.un.org/womenwatch/daw/cedaw/.

4th UN World Conference on Women in Beijing, and the subsequent Platform for Action. http://www.un.org/womenwatch/daw/beijing/platform/.

Rome Statute of the International Criminal Court. http://untreaty.un.org/cod/icc/index.html.

### On domestic violence:

Southall Black Sisters. http://www.southallblacksisters.org.uk/.

Refuge (U.K. organization for battered women). http://www.refuge.org.uk/.

The Family Justice Centre, 69 Park Lane, Croydon, Surrey CR0 1JD (020 8688 0100).

On domestic violence as it applies to women's immigration status:

Women's Aid. http://www.womensaid.org.uk/landing_page.asp?section =000100010000900050006.

On women and the environment:

Buckingham-Hatfield, Susan. *Gender and Environment*. London: Routledge, 2000.

Economy, Elizabeth. *The River Runs Black: The Environmental Challenge to China's Future*. Ithaca, N.Y.: Cornell University Press, 2005.

On women and war:

The Geneva Convention relative to the Treatment of Prisoners of War: http://www.unhchr.chhttp://www.icrc.org/Web/Eng/siteeng0.nsf/htmlall/genevaconventions.

For more information on French Muslim activist Samira Bellil and her work: Ni Putes Ni Soumises, www.niputesnisoumises.com; and Bellil, Samira *Dans l'enfer des tournantes* [In the Hell of Gang-Rapes], Paris: Denoël, 2003.

On prostitution:

The POPPY Project. http://www.eaves4women.co.uk/POPPY_Project/POPPY_Project.php.

Mainliners, U.K. charity working with drug users and sex workers. http://mainliners.org.uk/.

Justice for Women, feminist legal reform campaigning group. http://www.jfw.org.uk.

On inequality in women's pay:

Babcock, Linda, and Sara Laschever. *Women Don't Ask: Negotiation and the Gender Divide*. Princeton, N.J.: Princeton University Press, 2003.

The final report of the former U.K. Equal Opportunities Commission before it merged into the Commission for Equality and Human Rights was "The Gender Agenda: The Unfinished Revolution." July 2007.

www.equalityhumanrights.com/Documents/Gender/General%20
advice%20and%20information/EOC%20Gender%20agenda.pdf.

For up-to-date statistics on the numbers of women in national
parliaments:

Inter-Parliamentary Union. www.ipu.org/wmn-e/world.

# Index

*abaya*, 9
abduction, 28, 30, 49, 129, 131, 147. *See* trafficking
abortion, 48–9, 101–6
Abu Ghraib, 118
activism, 76, 153–62, 178
adultery, 61–68
advertising, 108, 127–28
Aethelbert law, 173–74
Afghanistan, 13, 40, 92, 117, 151, 162–63
Africa, 40, 70–71, 73, 83, 100–1, 103, 138, 147
African American women, 11, 87
agriculture, 134–36
Ahluwalia, Kiranjit, 88–89
Ahmadinejad, Mahmoud, 66, 168–69
Al-Attas, Huda, 23–24
al-Baz, Rania, 156, 158
Ali Zardari, Asif, 46
Amazons, 42
Amnesty International, 53, 55–56, 113
Amsterdam, 122, 166
ancient Greece, 165–66
Angola, 114
Annan, Kofi, xi
Anti-Slavery International, 28
Argentina, 42
arranged marriage, 48–49

Artemisia of Persia, 42
Asia, 25, 70, 73, 101, 109
Asian Women's Fund, 112
"asking for it," 9–10
asylum, 148–49
Asylum Aid, 148
Australia, 34, 65, 172

Ballard, Jim, 22–23
Banda, Hastings, 5–6
Bandaranaike, Solomon, 38
Bandaranaike, Srimavo, 38
Bangladesh, 39, 90, 139–41, 143–44
beauty and sexuality, 107
Beijing Platform, 103
Bellil, Samira, 9
Ben-Gurion, David, 37
Bhutan, 172
Bhutto, Benazir, 39, 45–46
Bindel, Julie, 124
Biro, Kathy, 31
birth control pill, 96, 98
bloggers, 158
boardroom politics, 34–36
Bolivia, 30
Borneo, 112
Bosnia, 114
Bosnia and Herzegovina, 117
Boudicca of the Iceni tribe, 42
Bowles, Hannah Riley, 32–33

Brazil, 58–59, 109
British Ministry of Defence, 119
Brunei, 172
Burkina Faso, 70–71
Burma, 39, 112
burqa, 40
Burrows, Eva, 30

Callipateira, 165–66
Cambodia, 104
Camp Victory, 118–19
Canada, 159–60, 172
Ceaucescu, Elena, 40
celebrity, 108, 120
Centers for Disease Control and
    Prevention, 90
CEOs, 34–35
Ceylon, 38
change, xii, 74–76, 153, 171–79.
    *See* legislation
Chechnya, 22
child labor, 29
child marriage, 15, 50, 81–2
child rearing, 14–15, 19, 31, 65
childbirth, 72, 77, 91–3
children, 54, 84–6, 92–3
Children and Armed Conflict,
    138
Chile, 104–5
China, xiv, 40, 42, 49, 109, 112,
    135
    one-child policy, 49
Ching, Jiang, 40
Chinkin, Christine, 139
"chores gap," 4
Christian marriage, 47
Christianity, 47
Ciccone, Madonna, 179
Civil Rights Act (1964), 155
civil rights movement, 153–5
cleaning. *See* housework
Cleopatra, 42

Clinton, Bill, 154
Clinton, Hillary, 40
clitoris, 71–72
collagen, 109
Collective of Men for Egalitarian
    Relationships (CORIAC),
    159–60
Colombia, 104–5
comfort women, 109–14
Commission for Equality and
    Human Rights (UK), 35
Commission on Human Rights
    and Administrative Justice
    (CHRAJ), 81
condoms, 97, 100–101
contraception, 95–101
Convention on the Elimination of
    All Forms of Discrimination
    against Women (CEDAW),
    176–77
Convention on the Nationality of
    Women, xiii
Coomaraswamy, Radhika, 138
Cooper, Charlotte, 166
Côte d'Ivoire, 76
Council of Europe, 132
crimes against humanity, 112,
    177–78
*The Crucible,* 78, 80
cuckold, 62

*Daily Mail,* 4
Darabi, Ali, 66
Darfur, 114, 149
daughters, 45–46, 48
Davidson, Emily, 172
De Wallen red-light district, 122
*Death Proof,* 126
deforestation, 135
Dellanian, Maureen, 96
Democratic Republic of Congo
    (DRC), 114–16, 162

dependence on men, 15, 19, 38,
    45, 81, 173
designer vaginas, 76–77
Diana, Princess of Wales, 47
diaphragm, 97
Diene, Rockaya, 74–75
Digitas, 31
Dinitz, Simcha, 37
discrimination, xiii-xiv, 14
divorce, 65, 67–69, 173–75
domestic sphere, 1–5, 14–19, 36,
    38, 45, 167
domestic violence, 20, 52–61, 73,
    133, 156–58
    definition of, 53
    and economic hardship, 55
    and failure of police, 56–57
    and fear, 54–55
    helplines, 60–61
    and safe centers, 58–59, 61
domestic workers, 24–30
*Domostroi*, 55
dowry, 46–48, 144
drawbridge mentality, 34
dress codes, 5–10, 23

early marriage, 15
Eastern Europe, 132
Ebadi, Shirin, 66
economic liberalization, 142
education,
    and women, xii, 1, 10–16, 31,
        38, 58, 80–81, 95, 136, 177
    and agriculture, 136
    barriers to, 14–16
    and development, 13–14
    history of, 11–13
    and prejudice, 15–16
    sex education, 95
    and witches, 80–81
Education for All, 13
Egypt, 42, 76, 158

El Moutawakel, Nawal, 165
El Salvador, 29, 104–6
Elizabeth I, 41–42
emergency medical centers, 58–59
England, 59
Entertainment Places Act
    (Thailand), 125
environment and gender, 134–38
environmental degradation, 134–
    35
environmental hazards, 135
Epsom Derby (1913), 171–72
Equal Opportunities
    Commission, 4, 32
Equal Pay Act, 155
Ethiopia, 15, 93, 95, 104
Europe, 78, 95–96, 114, 123,
    129, 146, 156, 160
European Union, 60–61
"evil stepmother," 67
exclusion, 42–43
executive positions, 33–36

Falklands War, 42
family law, 174–76
family planning clinics, 97
fathers, 19, 46–47, 164
fear, 23–24
female condom, 100–101
female genital mutilation (FGM),
    60, 69, 77, 99, 150
    and change, 74–75
    in hospitals, 75–76
female infanticide, 48–49
Femidom, 100–101
*The Feminine Mystique*, 155
femininity, 2–3, 30, 167
feminist movement, 155–56
Ferguson, Sarah, 47
Finnbogadóttir, Vigdís, 38
*Forbes*, 15
forced marriage, 50, 53

France, 6–7, 9, 50
Franjou, Marie-Hélène, 50
Friedan, Betty, 155

Gambaga witches, 80–81
Gandhi, Indira, 38–39
Gap-Soon, Choi, 111–12
gendered wages, 31–33
Geneva Conventions, 114–15,
146
Germany, 172
Ghana, 80–81, 136
glass ceilings, 33–35
glass cliff, 35–36
global gag rule, 103
globalization, 138–45
effects on women, 141–45
See textile worker
Gokaldas Exports, 139–40
Good Housewife Competition, 3
good woman, ideal of, 2–3, 15–
17
"gorno," 128–31
Gräfenberg, Ernst, 97
Grameen Bank, 143–44
Grand Theft Auto, 129
Great Britain, 3–4, 6–7, 11–12,
15–16, 22, 28, 31–32, 35,
41–42, 51, 53–55, 63, 84–
87, 96, 117, 119–21, 136,
167–68, 172–73
and adultery, 63
and domestic violence, 53–55
and gendered wages, 31–32
and military, 119
and prostitution, 120–21
and slavery, 28
and sport, 167–8
suffrage, 172
and women workers, 35
and women's prisons, 84–87
See Home Office

Green Belt Movement, 138
Grey-Thompson, Tanni, 170
Grindhouse, 126, 129
Guatemala, 20, 139, 156
murders, 20
Guerin, Veronica, 22
Gulf Cooperation Council, 26–27
Guthrie, Kate, 104

Hadith, 174
hair extensions, 109
"Hammer of Witches," 78
Haq Mehr, 175
Hargreaves, Alison, 22–23
Hawthorne, Nathaniel, 61–62
"headscarf debate," 6–9
Heraea Games, 166
Heyzer, Noeleen, 39
hijab (headscarf), 6–9
Hindu, 69, 81–82. See Sati
Hindu Succession Act, 81
Hindu Widows Remarriage Act,
81
Hinduja, Dinesh, 139–40
HIV/AIDS, 13, 26, 71–72, 83,
98–100, 115–16
and "cleansing" myth, 99–100
and contraception, 98–100
home. See domestic sphere
Home Office, 28, 53, 148
Honduras, 143
honor killings, 59–61
Hoon, Geoff, 117
Hoshi, Mohammad, 66
Hostel Part II, 128
household gardens, 135
housework, 2–4
Hudood Ordinance, 63–64
human rights, xi-xiii, 54, 73,
176–77
and domestic violence, 54
gender statistics, xi-xii

and UN Charter, xiii
*See* education
Human Rights Commission in
   Mexico, 29
Human Rights Watch, 84
husbands, 19, 26, 56, 82

Icaza, Emilio Alvarez, 29
Iceland, 38
incest, 26, 61, 104
income, 31
India, 5, 26–27, 48, 59, 81–83,
   125–26, 135, 137, 163–64,
   177
Indonesia, 6, 24–25, 27, 29, 112,
   136–37
infant mortality, 92–93
infibulation, 71–72
"inner inhibitor," 35
internal bra, 110
International Congress of
   Women, 160
International Federation of
   Journalists, 33
International Labour
   Organization (ILO), 29, 141
International Space Station, 36
International Suffrage Alliance,
   160
Internet, 142, 158
Internet pornography, 127–28
intrauterine device (IUD), 97
"invisible refugees," 145
invisibility of older women, 10
Iran, 9, 66, 158, 168–9
Iraq, xiv-xv, 22, 117–19, 145
Ireland, 104
Islam, 6–9, 59, 68
Islamic countries, 6–10, 23, 39,
   69, 164–65
Islamic fundamentalism, 8, 23
Islamic law, 63, 174–75. *See zina*

Islamic marriage certificate, 174–
   75
Israel, 42
International Olympic
   Committee, 166

Jalal, Massouda, 162–63
Jamaica, 40, 54
James, Henry, 12
Japan, 109–14
Japanese Imperial Army, 111
Jewish orthodoxy, 5
Jewish wedding service, 47
Joan of Arc, 44
Johnson-Sirleaf, Ellen, 40
Joshi, Sharu, 28
Joya, Malalai, 40
Jozana, Zamukulungisa, 78
Justice for Women, 124

Kadyrov, Ramzan, 22
Kahn, Aina, 174
Kakuma refugee camp, 149–50
Kanwar, Roop, 82
Karma Nirvana, 51
Karo-Kari, 60
Karpinski, Janis, 118–19
Karzai, Hamid, 162
Kaufman, Michael, 159
*kaytecyenza,* 101
Kenya, 67, 75–76, 99, 138, 147
Kenyan refugee camps, 147, 149–
   50
Ketubah, 47
Khada, Asma, 174
Khwaja, Imrana, 65
King, Billie Jean, 170
Kirkaldy, Irene Morgan, 153–54
Koran, 6, 68–69, 174
Koroma, Hannah, 70
Kosovo, 117
Kurdish refugees, 145

Kyi, Aung San Suu, 39

labial plastic surgery, 76–77
Latin America, 29–30, 59
Latina women, 87
leadership and women, 30,
    36–43
Lebanon, 172
legislation, xii-xiv, 30–31, 57–58,
    123–25, 153–56, 172–79
  progressive laws, 175–76
  women and the law, 173–75
  women as lawmakers, 176–77
  *See* Rome Statute
lesbians, 48, 87
Liberia, 40, 114, 163–64
*Lilya 4-Ever,* 132
liposelection, 110
Lockheed Aircraft Corporation,
    18
Loftus, Pamela, 76
Lomé Peace Accord, 161
The Long March, 91–92
Lord's Resistance Army, 114
Lucas, Robin, 87
Lyon, Juliet, 86

Maathai, Wangari, 138
Madadgaar Helpline, 60
Madame Mao, 40
Mainliners charity, 124
Malawi, 5–6, 83
Malaysia, 25, 52, 59, 112
Malé, Serge, 150
Mali, 94, 99
Malta, 104–5
Mao Zedong, 37
Marcos, Imelda, 40
marital rape, 50–52, 54
marriage, 45–52, 68–69, 174–75.
    *See* adultery; arranged
    marriage; child marriage;
divorce; forced marriage;
    marital rape; nationality
*Married Love,* 97
Married Women's Property Act
    (Britain), 173
Maranya, Julie, 75
Marshall, Thurgood, 154
Mason, Lisa, 120
maternal health, 91–96
maternal mortality, 93
Mauritania, 76
Mayanja, Rachel, 164
McCorvey, Norma, 102
Mehta, Deepak, 81
Meir, Golda, 37, 42, 179
Melroy, Pamela, 36–37
men's jobs, 17–18
Mexico, 139, 159–60
microcredit, 143–45
Middle East, 25, 59, 70, 73, 118,
    147, 158, 176
migrant workers, 142. *See*
    domestic workers
migration, 139, 141–42
military, 117–19
Miller, Arthur, 78–79
Miller, Portia Simpson, 40
"missing millions," 49
Moldova, 129–32
Monzon, Marielos, 156–58
Moodysson, Lucas, 132
Morgan, Robin, 30
Morocco, 6, 24, 164–65
Moscow Women's Crisis Center,
    56
mothers as domestic workers, 26
  and education, 13
  and encouragement, 23–24
  health of, 91–96
  idealization of, 2–3
  and prison, 84–86
  and refugees, 150

Mt. Everest, 22
Mullane, Frank, 57
Musharraf, Pervez, 60

Narayan, Prem, 82
National Association for the
    Advancement of Colored
    People (NAACP), 154
National Convention on Human
    Rights and Human Dignity
    (2000), 60
*National Law Journal,* 87–88
negotiating, and women, 32–33
National Garment Workers
    Federation, 141
National Health Service,
    148–49
nationality, xiii
natural disasters, 136–38
Nazer, Mende, 28
Nepal, 27–8, 171
the Netherlands, 121–23, 160
New Zealand, 172
Newbold, Yve, 34
Newell, Mike, 168
Ni Putes, Ni Soumises, 9
Nicaragua, 104–5
Nigeria, 83
Nikah Nameh, 175
*niqab* (full veil), 6
Noer, Michael, 15
nongovernmental organizations
    (NGOs), 33, 74, 84, 141,
    178
Norman Conquest (1066), 174

Obama, Barack, 103
Obama, Michelle, 40
Oberlin College, 11
*Offside,* 168–69
Olympics, 165–66
Oxford University, 11

Pacific Islands, 112
Paíz, Claudina Isabel Velázquez,
    20
Pakistan, 39, 45–46, 59–60, 63–
    64, 174. *See* Hudood
    ordinance
Palestinian women, 19–20
Palin, Sarah, 168
Pankhurst, Richard, xv
Pankhurst, Sylvia, xv
Paralympics, 170
Parks, Rosa, 154
Parton, Dolly, 107–8
Patterson, Mary Jane, 11
Pausanias, 165–66
peacekeepers, 160–64
pedophile internet sites, 128
Pemberton, Alan, 57
Pemberton, Julia, 56–57
Pemberton, William, 57
Penney, Angela, 58
Persian Gulf, 26
Philippines, 25, 40, 112, 120, 139
Phillips, Trevor, 35
Phumaphi, Joy, 93
plastic surgery, 76–77, 107–10
Plato, 10
Poland, 172
political office, 37–43
Politkovskaya, Anna, 21–22
pornography, 126–29, 155
post-conflict situations, 39, 150
poverty, and women, 31, 40,
    133–34, 142–45
power, 37–43
pregnancy, 92–3, 95, 115
primogeniture, 173
prison, 84–89
property, women as, 46–47, 56,
    58
prostitution, 38, 48, 111, 115,
    119–26, 131, 149, 165

Protocol to Prevent, Suppress, and Punish Trafficking in Persons, 132
public hangings, 66
public space, 16–24, 38, 144, 167
public women, 21–23
Punjab, 51

Quayson, Richard, 81
Quechua Indians, 30

Rajputs, 82
rape, xii, 9, 25, 50–52, 54, 61, 63–56, 87–88, 99–100, 104, 111–19, 130, 141, 147–48, 155, 159, 177–78
  and adultery, 63
  gang rape, 9
  within marriage, 50–52
  statistics on, xii
  and war, 111–19
  as war crime, 114–15
war statistics, 116–17
Rayner, Amy, 168
Reagan, Nancy, 40
Reagan, Ronald, 103
reconstruction, post-war, 162–63
refugees, women, 61, 114, 145–51
religion and divorce, 68–69
returnees, 149–50
Rodriguez, Casimira, 30
Roe, Jane, 101–2
Roe v. Wade, 101–2
Roman Catholic Church, 68–69, 119
Romania, 40
Rome Statute of the International Criminal Court, 115, 177–8
Ross, Tanya, 86
Roth, Eli, 128

Rousseau, Jean-Jacques, 2, 16–17, 19
Russia, 21–22, 55–56, 128, 132
Rwanda, 37, 39, 116, 176–78
Rwanda Inheritance Law, 176–7

Sadr, Shadi, 158
Safa, Afsanah, 7–8
Saint Augustine, 68
Salvation Army, 30
San Diego Family Justice Center, 59
Sanger, Margaret, 97
Sanghera, Jasvinder, 51
Sankara, Thomas, 70–71
Sankoh, Foday, 161–62
sari, 5
Sati, 82–83
Saudi Arabia, 9, 26–27, 156–58, 172
Scandinavia, 37, 156
selective abortion, 48–49
Sen, Amartya, 134
Senegal, 74–75
senior management positions, 33–36
September 11, 2001 (terrorist attacks), 54
Serbia, 117
Seventh International Conference of American States, xiii
sex industry, 119–26
sex tourism, 123
sexism, 155, 167–68
sexual abuse, 26, 148, 159
sexual availability, culture of, 95–96
sexual assault, 53, 116, 118
sexual exploitation, 13, 27
sexual harassment, 14, 117, 159
sexual slavery, 111–13, 115–16, 129–32. See trafficking

sexual violence and dress, 9–10
  and Guatemala, 20
  *See* comfort women; rape;
    Rome Statute
Shahaaleh, Atefeh Rejabi, 66
Sharia. *See* Islamic law
Shakespeare, William, 47–48
Sierra Leone, 70, 92, 116, 161–62
Sigurdadottir, Johanna, 38
Sikhism, 59, 69
Singapore, 112
slavery, 24–30. *See* sexual slavery
"soccer moms," 168
Somali refugees, 147
Sonagachi project (India), 125–26
South Africa, 77–78, 99, 104
South Asia, 13, 26, 38, 59, 136–
    37
South Asian tsunami (2004),
    136–38
Southeast Asia, 134–35
Soviet Union, 55, 172
space, 36–37
Spain, 59
spectatorship, 168–69
spinsters, 48
*Spitting Image,* 41
sports, 164–69
Sports Journalist Association of
    Great Britain, 167–68
Sri Lanka, 25–26, 38, 137, 139
stalking, 53
"sticky floors," 30–37
Stopes, Marie, 97
sub-Saharan Africa, 84
Sudan, 28, 114, 140, 149–50
suffrage, 171–72
suicide, 50
surrogate power, 38–39, 40–41
Suarez, Cristina, 25
*The Sun,* 127
survival sex, 149

Sweden, 92, 123–25, 156
Switzerland, 104
Syria, 42

Tamils, 26
*The Taming of the Shrew,* 47–48
Tarantino, Quentin, 126, 128
Taylor, Diane, 124
technology, 158
Telford, John, 145
textile workers, 139–41
Thailand, 125, 147
Thapa, Ratna Maya, 171
Thatcher, Margaret, 41–42
threadlift, 110
Tostan, 74
Toubia, Nahid, 70
trafficking, 29, 49, 115, 121, 123,
    125, 129–32, 142
transactional sex, 149
trees, 138
Trung sisters, 42
Tuareg tribe, 94
Tunisia, 175–76
Turkey, 8, 60–61

Uganda, 67–68, 114
UNESCO, 13
United Arab Emirates (UAE), 25–
    27
United Kingdom, 11, 35, 50–52,
    57, 84–89, 95, 100, 103–4,
    120–21, 124, 127, 148, 163,
    168, 174–75
  abortion statistics, 103–4
  peace activism, 163
  and prostitution, 120–1
  and refugees, 148
  and teenage pregnancy, 95
United Kingdom Prison Reform
    Trust, 86
United Nations, xi, xiii, 132

UN Charter, xiii
UN Children's Fund (UNICEF), 60
UN Convention on the Elimination of All Forms of Discrimination against Women (CEDAW), xiii-xiv
UN Declaration on the Elimination of Violence against Women, 52
UN Development Fund for Women (UNIFEM), 28, 39, 144, 173
UN female peacekeepers, 163–64
UN High Commissioner for Refugees (UNHCR), 145–7, 149–50
UN Security Council, 151
UN Security Council Resolution 1325, 163–64
UN World Conference on Human Rights (Vienna), 73
UN World Conference on Women (Beijing), xiv, 43
United States, 11, 15, 30, 34, 36–37, 40, 54, 86–87, 97–98, 101–3, 117–20, 128, 155–56
    and abortion, 101–3
    and commodification of sex, 119–20
    and contraception, 97–98
    gun culture, 54
    lack of paid maternity leave, 156
    and pedophile websites, 128
    women's prison statistics, 86–87
    *See* civil rights movement; feminist movement
U.S. Army, and women, 117–19
U.S. Congress, 155

U.S. Constitution, 102
U.S. cruise missiles, 163
U.S. Space Shuttle Discovery, 36–37
U.S. Supreme Court, 102, 154
Universal Declaration of Human Rights, 49, 92
Uruguay, xiii

Vietnam, 42
*A Vindication of the Rights of Women,* 12
violence, xi-xii, xiv, 9–10, 20, 40, 49, 52–61, 80–81
    and dress codes, 9–10
    honor-based, 53.
    *See* domestic violence; female genital mutilation; sexual violence

Wade, Henry, 102
Wages. *See* gendered wages
war, 109–19
war crimes, 112, 114–15, 177–78
War on Want, 141
*Water,* 81
Western culture, 9, 108, 119–21, 127
Western romantic novel, 47
White Ribbon Campaign (Canada), 159–60
Whitson, Peggy, 36–37
widow cleansing, 83–84
widows, 81–84, 133, 166
Wimbledon prize money, 169–70
witches, 48, 77–81
witch hunts, 78–79
wives, 45–46, 56, 84
Wollstonecraft, Mary, 2, 12
women and war, 109–19 statistics, 116–17

Women's Caucus for Gender
Justice, 115
Women's International League for
Peace and Freedom, 160
women's police stations, 58–59
Women's Protection Bill
(Pakistan), 64
women's rights, xii-xiv, 73, 76, 91,
97, 115, 123–25, 143, 153,
158, 177–79
and birth control, 97
and technology, 158
and women's health, 91
*See* activism; female genital
mutilation; legislation; Rome
Statute
women's shelters, 55, 130–32
workforce, and women, 31–36
working outside the home, 17–20

World Bank, 136
World's Fair Exhibition, 166
World Health Organization, 71,
93, 103
World War I, 17, 109, 160
World War II, 17–18, 41, 109–
11. *See* comfort women
worldwide abortion facts, 103–4

Yemen, 23, 76
Yom Kippur War, 42
Yugoslavia, 178
Yunus, Muhammad, 143

Zambia, 83
Zia, Khaleda, 39
Zia ul-Haq, Muhammad, 63
Zimbabwe, 101
*zina,* 63–64